June 16, 1994

With appreciation for the Pacific Institute's influence on South College and your 1994 Commencement Address.

John T. South III
President

SAVANNAH

Crown of the Colonial Coast

CORPORATE PROFILES
BY POLLY POWERS STRAMM

ART DIRECTOR
ANNE CASTRODALE

TOWERY PUBLISHING INC.

by Martha Giddens Nesbit

CREATIVE DIRECTOR
BRIAN GROPPE

PHOTOGRAPHY EDITOR
JOSEPH BYRD

MEMPHIS, TENNESSEE 1992

Library of Congress Cataloging-in-Publication Data

Nesbit, Martha Giddens.
    Savannah : crown of the colonial coast / Martha Giddens Nesbit :
corporate profiles by Polly Powers Stramm.
      p.   cm. — (Urban tapestry series)
    Includes index.
    ISBN 0-9628128-7-0 : $39.50
      1. Savannah (Ga.)—History. 2. Savannah (Ga.)—Pictorial works.
3. Savannah (Ga.)—Industries.   I. Stramm, Polly Powers, 1954-   .
II. Title.   III. Series.
F294.S2N47   1992
975.8'724—dc20   92-53586
                                                        CIP

SAVANNAH: CROWN OF THE COLONIAL COAST
Copyright ©1992 by Towery Publishing, Inc.

TOWERY PUBLISHING, INC.
1835 Union Avenue, Suite 142, Memphis, Tennessee 38104

Publisher: J. Robert Towery
Editor: Patricia M. Towery
Managing Editor: Michael C. James
Assistant Editor: Allison Jones Simonton
Profile Art Director: Jil M. Foutch
Editorial Consultant: Barbara P. Heuer

*Preceding pages: anchor—Joseph Byrd; heron chick—Gregory M. Williams; stained glass window—Steve Bisson,
Savannah News-Press; and garden statue—Linda Erzinger.*

SAVANNAH

A little boy dances on a snail in one of Savannah's lovely, but hidden, walled gardens, like this one on East Jones Street.

Acknowledgments

In the summer of 1991, I accepted the assignment to write the narrative for a book on Savannah, flattered but confident that I was equal to the task. I had, after all, lived in the city 17 years, interviewed hundreds of people through my association with *The Savannah Morning News*, and developed a network of sources through civic work.

What I discovered as I began to dig, however, was that what I thought I knew about this city was not enough. Through research, referrals, and hundreds of hours on the telephone, I met new and fascinating people who shared their knowledge, memories, and expertise about Coastal Georgia. It is these people, most of whom are not otherwise mentioned in this book, who helped to shape a narrative that, I hope, looks at who we are, why we are, what we do, and, most especially, why we choose to do it here.

John Crawford, a marine science educator at the University of Georgia Marine Extension Service, provided hours of information on the environment. Charles Samz, a retired geophysicist and self-styled naturalist, added anecdotes to that information. Pat Metz, refuge ranger for the Savannah Coastal Refuges, discussed birds and wildlife. Edie Schmidt, an artist with the University of Georgia Marine Extension Service, provided information on Savannah's prehistory. Don Gardner, director of Savannah's Park and Tree Commission, answered endless questions on the city squares.

Leslie Gordon, now deputy director of the Cultural Olympiad for the Atlanta Committee for the Olympic Games, influenced the section on arts in Savannah. Elinor Minshew, vice president of the Savannah Economic Development Authority, provided assistance in the economic portions of the book. David T. Geurnsey Jr., the executive director of the Ships of the Sea Museum, who also lectures on the development of the port, was immensely generous with his time and expertise about matters along the Savannah River. Armstrong State College history professor John D. Duncan was an excellent telephone editor for the history section. Stephanie Churchill, director of Historic Savannah Foundation, was a reliable source for preservation questions. Beth Reiter of the Metropolitan Planning Commission was a superb counsel on historic matters. Architect and friend Jerry Miller made accessible a collection of architectural books. *Savannah News-Press*

columnist and colleague Tom Coffey helped steer me to the influential people who shaped Savannah's past.

Working behind the scenes to double-check facts and dates were reference librarians at the Chatham County Public Library and the Georgia Historical Society, as well as the librarians at the *Savannah News-Press*. The Savannah Area Chamber of Commerce was always ready to supply information as well.

Before beginning this project, I re-read *A Guide to the Georgia Coast* by the Georgia Conservancy, *Guale, the Golden Coast of Georgia* published by Friends of the Earth, *The Ogeechee—a River and Its People* by Jack Leigh, *Historic Savannah* by Malcolm Bell, and the wonderful *Savannah Revisited* by Mills B. Lane. The feelings of those authors are often reflected in this narrative.

Working with my associates on this project—Cindy Meyer, longtime friend Polly Powers Stramm, and Joseph Byrd—could not have been more pleasant.

On a personal level, my husband, Gary, was tolerant of meatless meals, and my two small sons, Zack and Emory, were mostly forgiving when trips to the beach and park had to be put on hold. Their sitter, Cynthia Davis, gamely went on bicycle rides to keep the children busy, and friends offered to take them for an hour or two on important deadline days. For your tolerance and support, I thank you.

Over the last year, I have become immensely dependent on the telephone, Federal Express, and my editor, Patty Towery, who provided encouragement, good judgment, and good humor throughout the editing process.

Because of my association with this book, I now look at Savannah with new eyes. I am happier than ever that we have chosen to live in this lovely, eccentric place we now consider home.

Martha Giddens Nesbit
September 1992

7

To appreciate the Lowcountry, one only needs a deserted porch, like this one at Officer's Row on Tybee Island, and a few quiet moments to drink in the view: acres and acres of marsh grass, clumps of live oaks, and an abundance of water.

Foreword

People who have visited Savannah's downtown Historic District believe they have seen a remarkable American city. They are absolutely correct.

But, unless they have gone past downtown and into the outlying neighborhoods, or visited one of several coastal island communities, or walked the beach of a barrier island inhabited mostly by wildlife, or watched the sun sink over the marsh on a late summer afternoon, they cannot fully appreciate the coastal way of life.

People who love Savannah like to tell stories about the visitors who come to the area for the first time and never leave. Many feel, with good reason, that this is a special place of great natural beauty and great historical significance. And of great promise.

Some may complain, legitimately, that progress is slow along the Georgia coast. But Savannah's reluctance to change too quickly has made it a city writers like to write about, tourists like to visit, and natives can't seem to stray too far from.

And change has come: The restoration of Savannah's historic treasures. Renewed appreciation and protection of the area's glorious natural environment. A new attitude about the public school system. Unified efforts to address the problems of disadvantaged youth. An aggressive campaign to bring in new business and provide jobs. Excitement over Savannah's critical role in the 1996 Olympic games.

These enormous accomplishments have been rewarded by a renewed sense of pride, national honors, and increasing numbers of pleasantly surprised visitors.

Life can seem relaxed along the Georgia coast, especially during the long, steamy summer. But things are never, ever dull.

Settings

We had been out in a little jon boat—a small, flat-bottomed, shallow-sided boat—for the better part of a hot, hazy afternoon, positioning the hull as far up in a tidal creek as it could go without getting stuck in the gray-black muck that covers the creek bottom and banks. We arrived two hours before low tide, the preferred time to go crabbing since we could catch crabs as they were swept up in the outgoing current and catch them again when the tide turned and the saltwater moved back into the creek.

We like to crab with hand lines for the sport of it; traps are too easy. Chicken backs or necks, allowed to ripen in the hot sun, are tied or pinned to the end of a long line of string weighted down with a chunk of lead. The lines are lowered over the side of the boat, and then you wait, but not very long. The string begins to twitch, or maybe it crawls away, sometimes with great intensity. That's the signal to pull the line in through your fingers, swiftly but cautiously, taking care not to jiggle or jerk. At the end, holding on to the chicken neck with great determination, is a blue crab. Unaware of what is to happen next, the crab does not let go, even as you scoop him up in a shallow net to deposit him in a five-gallon bucket, where he joins dozens more.

With two buckets full, we decide to stop, content with the knowledge that, in a few hours, we will be back home, showered and fresh, feasting on boiled crabs and butter. But now, our backs are rust-colored from too much sun and stiff from the constant crouching. Mud is splattered on the sides of the boat, on our T-shirts and cut-offs, in our hair and across our faces, smeared there in a feeble attempt to hold off an army of biting sand gnats.

Our lips are parched and salty.

We sit back in silence to enjoy the twilight glow as the marsh settles into evening. The crabs occasionally flail their claws, scratching against the sides of the buckets. Yellow rays filter through lime green marsh grass and fall, glistening, on the ripples of the blue-green saltwater. A pelican dives for its supper. A fish jumps. An egret, startled by some invisible sound, flaps its wings with great effort before lifting its snow-white body from the marsh mud.

A peace settles in, and we breathe a gentle sigh of wonder at the beauty that has been bestowed upon the Georgia coast.

Crabbing is one of the best ways to understand the hold the coast has on the people who live here. Once crabbing is in your blood, it is hard to imagine living too far from the creeks and rivers that offer this particular pleasure.

Another way is taking a slow walk downtown through the squares, leisurely reading the raised letters of the monuments that tell the Savannah story. So, too, is sitting on a bench on River Street, watching ships make their way cautiously up the Savannah River.

"Savannah is the most beautiful city," says Mary Helen Ray, chairman of the Park and Tree Commission, a person whose efforts in protecting trees brought her the 1992 Joyce Kilmer Award from the National Arbor Day Foundation. "There are older cities, and more successful ones, economically, but Savannah is the most beautiful."

Savannahians like to show off their city, their marshes, and islands. They take pleasure in being tour guides, taking newcomers to the places they love best.

Savannahians brag about the downtown district, about the number and uniformity of the preserved structures, punctuated by precious jewels of notable design. They take pride in the city's history and the fact that so much of it can be experienced by visiting museum houses, monuments, churches, and forts. They never tire of showing off the city squares, spacious and green, which are part of a unique plan that has survived 250 years. Environmentalists boast of the barrier islands, of the abundant wildlife and sea creatures, and talk of the delicate balance of nature that must be maintained in our marshes.

But it is the water that is Savannah's lifeblood—from the Atlantic Ocean to the two primary rivers, the commercial Savannah and the pristine Ogeechee, to the hundreds of tidal creeks that run their fingers through miles of marsh grass. These waters provide an environment sustaining a food chain of global importance and make possible a thriving international shipping business. They offer a natural playground for those who love water recreation, not to mention spectacular settings for those who simply want to take in the view.

And regardless of its many other attributes, it is Savannah's prime location with access to ocean waters that has brought about the city's prized role in the 1996 Olympic Games. For 17 days in July and August of that year, sailing competitions will take place in the waters around Savannah, exposing the area to 40 percent of the world's population—3 billion people—who will be watching the events on television.

The water, it seems, is at the very heart of what makes life in Savannah so appealing. Therefore, we begin our exploration of Savannah at the banks of the Savannah River, a swiftly moving ribbon of water that begins at the Hartwell Dam in Augusta and snakes its way 314 miles to the Atlantic Ocean, forming a natural boundary between South Carolina and Georgia.

The part of the river that is open to commercial traffic ranges from 500 to 700 feet in width and is dredged to a depth of 38 feet, with plans to increase that depth to 42 feet to accommodate even larger container ships. More than 1,500 vessels—some as long as 1,000 feet—glide soundlessly down the Savannah River each year, providing a spellbinding sight to spectators on shore. The ships' course from the Atlantic Ocean is 24 miles from the Tybee jetties to the terminals operated by the Georgia Ports Authority. On the way, in full view of their River Street audiences, the ships must pass under a magnificent new bridge of concrete and cables that took three years and $70 million to build.

"I think it is perhaps the most amazing sight of all in Savannah to see the ships coming down the river. They are coming here from far away, and they are going somewhere far away. You put yourself on these ships, and it's mystical to think of where you will end up," says Tony Cope, a native Savannahian whose ancestors came here in 1743.

Strolling down the riverfront, it is easy to envision life in Savannah as it was in the mid-1800s. By that time, Savannah had become an important seaport shipping buckskin, cotton, pine rosin, lumber, and rice to England, as well as New York, Philadelphia, Baltimore, Boston, Charleston, and the West Indies.

Cotton eventually became the dominant export crop, and for more than a century—from the invention of the cotton gin in 1793 to the collapse of the cotton culture in the early 1900s—the cotton trade made immense fortunes for planters, merchants, and shipping magnates. In the mid-1800s, only two places in the world

quoted the price for cotton: Liverpool, England and Savannah.

Cotton merchants built imposing brick warehouses five stories high along the river at the foot of the bluff, from which they could watch their bales being loaded and unloaded. Their offices, connected to Bay Street by bridges and cast-iron arches, became known as "Factors' Row" or "Factors' Walk." Although most of the warehouses became dilapidated with time, many were still standing in 1977 when $7 million in private, city, and federal money was spent to revitalize the area. Today, remarkably enough, exteriors of the warehouses remain unchanged; the interiors are often altered only slightly to accommodate the more than 75 boutiques, gift shops, restaurants, taverns, studios, and museums housed along the river.

Ballast stones that line the ramps and embankments along the riverfront make walking in heels a miserable task, but they offer old-world charm and a historical footnote. The stones were used as ballast to control the draft of 18th and 19th century sailing ships and discarded along the sandy banks once new cargo was taken on. They serve as a reminder of the longtime vitality of the river and its importance in the city's prosperous past.

It is the water that is Savannah's lifeblood— from the Atlantic Ocean to the two primary rivers, the commercial Savannah and the pristine Ogeechee, to the hundreds of tidal creeks that run their fingers through miles of marsh grass.

THE SQUARES

South of the riverfront are the historic city squares, which are surely one of the reasons *Walking Magazine* proclaimed Savannah in 1991 as one of the top-10 walking cities in America. The squares have also been designated as a National Historic Civil Engineering Landmark.

Savannah was founded by James Edward Oglethorpe, a member of British Parliament and a military man to the core. Oglethorpe's design laid out a series of wards and squares, with each ward of 40 lots planned around a square flanked on two sides by four trust lots reserved for public buildings. The squares were where neighbors could gather socially and for protection if Savannah was attacked. Subsequent city leaders continued Oglethorpe's design, and by the mid-1800s, there were 24 squares in all, with a large green space, Forsyth Park, developed in 1851 at the end of Bull Street.

Today, 21 of the 24 squares have been refurbished, groomed, and planted in a living pattern that surely

Oglethorpe would have approved of, thanks in large part to the city's Park and Tree Commission. Each square has a name, and no two squares are alike in detail or in theme. Plentiful benches provide perches for lunch or contemplation. Monuments to the people who influenced Savannah's history are at the heart of many.

Most remarkably, you can stand at the southernmost square, Monterey, and have visual contact with the northernmost square, Johnson. The result is the feeling of a city built within a large park rather than of small unrelated parks positioned between buildings.

Tourists are generally amazed by the variety of flora that flourishes in Savannah's sub-tropical climate. Liriope, mondo, ajuga, and English ivy cover the ground. Azalea, camellia, Indian hawthorn, yaupon holly, and shillings holly provide a green backdrop and splashes of color. Live oak, magnolia, sabal palm, crape myrtle, and dogwood offer shade and contour. Twisting up tree trunks and cascading over garden walls are romantic climbers: wisteria, Cherokee rose, and Virginia creeper.

The Spanish moss that seems to drape from every available tree branch is a bromeliad—a member of the pineapple family—that flowers in June with green petals. It does not choke the tree, as is sometimes thought; it is an air plant, not a parasite. Nor does it contain bugs, unless it lies around on the ground long enough to become a home for them. In the mid- and late-19th century, Spanish moss was gathered and boiled with chemicals, and the remaining fiber was used to stuff mattresses and upholstered furniture. Even earlier, Indian women used moss fibers to make clothing. Today, Spanish moss is important to coastal birds, who fancy it for their nests.

City forebears went out of their way to plant an urban forest that provides beauty, shade, and brilliant light shows on sunny days. Although a few live oaks have survived several hundred years, the area's first urban forest of pines was mostly lost in 1804 during a force-five hurricane. There followed a major planting of live oaks, southern magnolia, and sabal palmetto in the late 1800s and early 1900s. Today's citizens are reaping the benefits of these magnificent 100-year-old trees, which must be continually maintained and replaced if Savannah is to retain its claim as "The Forest City."

Forsyth Park, five squares from the Savannah River, is a testament to the pleasure and purpose of green space: 31 acres, seeded with rye during winter months, provide a year-round green setting for scampering squirrels and pesky pigeons, as well as for children who swing from playground equipment and splash in city-provided wading pools. The park is often a frenzy of outdoor activity, with walking, frisbee-throwing, soccer, football, and tennis taking place simultaneously.

Located at the heart of the park is a cast-iron fountain erected in 1858 in a design similar to the grand Paris fountain in the Place de la Concorde. The fountain was renovated in 1988 through a community-wide effort. Within the park's borders are the Marine Memorial, the Confederate Memorial, the Spanish-American War Memorial, and the Fragrant Garden for the Blind, planted by the Garden Clubs of Savannah in 1963, the first such garden in the southeastern United States. And somewhere in the park, protected by their obscurity, are two Franklinia—extinct in nature—small, delicate, picky trees named after American statesman Benjamin Franklin.

HISTORIC ARCHITECTURE

Surrounding and spreading beyond the squares are gracious homes remarkable for their continuity of style. Many of the earliest buildings were destroyed in a great fire of 1796; others were lost through storms and neglect. However, thousands more dating from the late 1700s to the mid-1800s remain, and it is this collection of structures that attracts so many visitors today.

Because of Oglethorpe's city plan, lots were narrow and deep, and what developed in the oldest areas of the city were row houses that sometimes ran continuously for a whole block. They were, in general, simple, symmetrical, and durable, constructed by master builders of wood, brick, and stone. Row houses typically were raised a story off the ground, with high stoops and walled gardens in back. A carriage house and servants' quarters were placed at the rear of the lot, accessible to the alley behind.

In among the sturdy, charming row houses are also examples of fine architecture: public buildings and mansions owned by what were once called "merchant princes."

William Jay, a young English architect, was lured to Savannah in 1817 by wealthy patrons who wanted the city to benefit from his talent. Jay brought the Regency style of architecture to Savannah, and possibly to America. Three examples of his work are owned by the Telfair Academy of Arts and Sciences, the city's major art museum: the Richardson-Owens-Thomas House, possibly the best preserved and finest example of his work in the nation, now run as a house museum; the Alexander Telfair house, the official residence of the governors of Georgia from 1760 until the end of the Revolutionary War, now operated as the Telfair

Since the earliest years, Savannahians have been partial to ornamental iron, molding it into fences and railings, fanciful downspouts, and decorative garden gates. These designs, in turn, have been enhanced by climbing vines that proliferate in the subtropical climate.

Academy art museum; and the William-Scarbrough House, where President James Monroe stayed during a 1819 visit. The Telfair acquired the house in 1991 and plans are being developed for its future use.

New Yorker John S. Norris designed the Green-Meldrim House—headquarters for General Sherman during his Civil War stay—in Gothic revival style. The sumptuous residence now serves as the parish house for St. John's Episcopal Church.

Savannah's Historic District is now one of the nation's largest historic urban landmark districts, including more than 2,300 architecturally and historically significant buildings in a 2.5-square-mile area.

It took the threatened demolition of one of these stately old mansions to solidify Savannah's fragmented preservation movement. In 1954, a handful of friends, distressed over the leveling of City Market on Ellis Square, raised enough capital to buy and spare the threatened Davenport House, built by master builder Isaiah Davenport in 1820. The group became Historic Savannah Foundation Inc., a private, non-profit organization dedicated to preservation and design, helping architects and residents blend new structures successfully with the old. The Davenport House was restored and opened as a house museum in 1962.

Savannah's Historic District is now one of the nation's largest historic urban landmark districts, including more than 2,300 architecturally and historically significant buildings in a 2.5-square-mile area.

The Victorian District has not yet experienced the revival that has taken place in the Historic District. The Victorian influence—identified by gingerbread trim, turrets, and gabled roofs—began in the mid-1800s and affected a large area of development south of the Historic District. Unfortunately, this area is Savannah's most neglected, and although it represents another great opportunity to salvage historic homes, at present many are in terrible condition and some are abandoned.

However, interest in the area is picking up: Individuals and churches in the neighborhood have completed isolated renovations, and applications for city and federal funds to finance home improvement loans doubled in 1992.

BEYOND DOWNTOWN

As fond as Savannahians are of the downtown area, they relish the chance to show off neighborhoods that tourists rarely see. Leaving the well-manicured squares of the Historic District and driving past the worn structures of the Victorian District brings you to Savannah's first suburbs. Ardsley Park and Chatham Crescent comprise 400 acres of impressive homes in various architectural styles, situated in a grid layout—perhaps a modern version of Oglethorpe's city plan.

Developed between 1910 and 1920, the area is an example of an early 20th century suburb in Georgia, a distinction that has placed it on the National Register of Historic Places.

Washington Avenue, located in the heart of the neighborhood, is a street of classic homes divided by a median of live oaks. It may be one of the most beautiful avenues in the area, especially during the early spring when fuchsia azaleas and white dogwoods offer their dazzling displays.

Victory Drive, a memorial to Savannah casualties of World War I, is enhanced by a palmetto-lined median and flanked on both sides by stately homes. It was the setting in 1910 and 1911 for two significant automobile races: The Grand Prix and The Vanderbilt Cup. The oaks that line the three-mile drive were top cut at 12 feet, which resulted in a lovely cathedral arch—a bit impractical in modern times with the proliferation of 13-foot trucks.

On the east end, Victory Drive becomes a busy thoroughfare that hasn't quite found its character. In one of the ironies of progress, several of the finest live oaks and palms on the drive were sacrificed for a much-needed overpass currently under construction. But thanks to the efforts of preservationists, the trees will be replaced when work is completed.

Just outside the city limits, still heading east, Victory Drive passes over the Wilmington River. A look to the right, down River Drive, reveals the tiny town of Thunderbolt, Georgia, where generations of shrimpers have kept their boats, earned their livelihoods, and fed seafood lovers throughout the South.

ISLAND LIFE

Victory Drive gradually turns into Highway 80, or Tybee Road. The 18-mile scenic drive from Savannah to Tybee skirts past Wilmington Island, Talahi Island, and a number of new island communities that have experienced booming growth in recent years.

Then, abruptly, the neighborhoods end, the road narrows, and Highway 80 becomes a heavenly strip of asphalt bordered on either side by rippling creeks, swaying marsh, drifting shrimp boats, and dramatic islands of oaks, cedars, and palms.

The drive runs into Tybee Island, two-and-a-half miles long and two-thirds of a mile wide, a little slice of sand that has served Savannahians for more than 150 years as a spot for picnicking, sailing, and swimming.

A Tybee lighthouse has guarded the Savannah River since 1736. Two hotels were constructed on Tybee in the mid-1800s, and summer cottages appeared soon after, first along the Back River, then along the beach, and finally at the south end. Much of what was erected on Tybee was destroyed in 1881 during a hurricane that submerged the island, but islanders soon began to rebuild.

A railroad even linked Savannah to Tybee as early as 1887 and was heavily used until 1933, when it was finally put out of business by the increased use of a highway built in 1923. The new road was filled with Savannahians who frequented the popular Tybrisa pavilion, where many of the big-name bands of the swing era got their start—Bob Crosby and Tommy Dorsey among others.

Tybee today is a community of homes, clubs, restaurants, amusement parks, and gift shops catering to tourism, which is the town's primary industry. The island's year-round residents seem pleased by the fact that family-owned cottages still greatly outnumber the condominiums.

Nine miles from Savannah is another island community, Isle of Hope, settled in 1736 by colonists Noble Jones, John Fallowfield, and Henry Parker, who were each given a grant of 500 acres. Jones established a plantation called Wormsloe, today the oldest plantation in Georgia continuously owned by one family. Although most of its land has been acquired by the state and Wormsloe is open to the public, Jones' descendants still live in the plantation house, built in 1828.

For many years, the Isle of Hope Methodist Church—a simple white frame structure on winding Parkersburg Road—was the only church on the island. During General Sherman's occupation of Savannah, Union soldiers camped in the Methodist churchyard. The sanctuary served as a hospital for Confederate soldiers, and those who died are buried in the churchyard.

Isle of Hope became the popular place for Savannahians, wilted by the city's summer heat, to cool off. They built summer houses along the bluff that faces the Skidaway River and enjoyed a relaxed lifestyle that included crabbing and berry-picking as major activities.

The drive down Bluff Drive is one of the most scenic in the area, with well-maintained antebellum houses showing off wide porches built to provide cross ventilation and catch the river breezes. Moss dangles from giant oaks—some as old as 250 years—and

wooden docks dot the river, marsh grass dancing on the other side.

Skidaway Island, eight miles long and three miles wide, lies south of the mouth of the Savannah River, protected by barrier islands Tybee, Wassaw, and Ossabaw. This area was inhabited by colonial settlers who built large plantations with romantic names: Modena, Little Comfort, and Seaside. But the island was inexplicably abandoned, the plantations going to ruin.

Skidaway Island slept quietly, undisturbed, for years. Then, in the late 1960s, Union Camp, a kraft paper manufacturing firm that owned vast acres of Southern pines, enlisted the help of The Branigar Organization to develop the island as a private residential community, while leaving much of the wild beauty of the place unspoiled.

Branigar's Master Plan called for limiting the number of homes to no more than one per half-acre and leaving almost half of the land for golf fairways, parks, and green space. In 1986, the plan won the Urban Land Institute's Award for Excellence, the Oscar for planned communities. The community is called The Landings at Skidaway, with more than 3,000 families in residence today.

During the 1996 Olympics, when Savannah hosts the yachting competitions, Priest's Landing at Skidaway Island will be the site of the marina. The Olympic Village will be built across the Wilmington River at the Sheraton Savannah Resort.

The University of Georgia Marine Extension Service Aquarium, which exhibits over 200 live animals representing 50 species of fish and invertebrates, is also located on Skidaway Island. The Marine Extension Service houses lecture rooms, labs, a dormitory, and cafeteria, where students from throughout the Southeast come to learn about marine life. The aquarium shares a campus with the Skidaway Institute of Oceanography, supported by the University Board of Regents. Scientists there are engaged in environmental and marine research utilized by scientists throughout the world.

White-tailed deer are plentiful in the thick underbrush of Skidaway Island. Atlantic bottlenose dolphin often play alongside shrimp boats and pleasure boats navigating ocean waters and the Intracoastal Waterway.

Alligators abound at the 26,000-acre Savannah National Wildlife Refuge, 15 minutes from downtown Savannah, the largest of seven refuges in the area. Over

260 species of birds have been recorded at the refuge, including the endangered peregrine falcon and southern bald eagle. Freshwater impoundments—working rice fields up until 1898—are attractive to a number of species of ducks. Because the refuge is located on the Atlantic Flyway, it also becomes a temporary resting spot for a variety of songbirds—primarily warblers and thrushes—that winter in Central and South America and the Caribbean.

At Oatland Island Education Center, located on a marsh island just east of Savannah, more than 50,000 students and adults each year take advantage of the 60-acre forest of nature trails that features natural habitats for indigenous Georgia wildlife: pelicans, herons, egrets, alligators, otters, deer, timber wolves, and the Eastern Woods Bison, now extinct in the Georgia wild. Perhaps the most unique feature of Oatland, which is owned and operated by the Savannah-Chatham public school system, is that all of the habitats, trails, the 500-foot marsh walkway, and docks were built by young people. Unique also is the admission charge: a can of Alpo dog food, which means that no school funds are spent for animal food.

Of all the magnificent wildlife that congregates along Georgia's coastal beaches, it is the sea turtle that perhaps best illustrates the area's dedication to preserving its natural heritage.

The loggerhead sea turtle (Caretta caretta), the only one of Georgia's four native sea turtles to regularly nest here, was placed on the Threatened Species list in 1978. In 1973, The Savannah Science Museum, in cooperation with the U.S. Fish and Wildlife Service and the Wassaw Island Trust, began the Caretta Research Project, conducted on the Wassaw Island National Wildlife Refuge each year from May through September, when loggerheads nest.

Through this project volunteer observers are offered a view of a prehistoric ritual performed almost every night in June and July: Huge loggerhead sea turtles—weighing from 150 to 300 pounds—struggle onto the hard packed sand to dig nests and deposit a clutch of about 124 golf ball-sized eggs before returning to the sea. During the nesting season, turtle researchers patrol the coast all night to mark and safeguard the precious contents of the loggerheads' nests. At one time, nearly 90 percent of all loggerhead eggs failed to hatch;

The marshes, according to scientists, are the richest acreage on the planet, and Georgia has more than any other state on the Atlantic coast—701,000 acres of salt marsh, mud flats, and swamps. Indeed, the word "Savannah" is a variation of the spelling of "savanna," or grassland.

however, thanks to the Caretta volunteers, nest loss on Wassaw Island has been all but eliminated.

THE OGEECHEE RIVER

Although much of the coast near Savannah is marshland, the area has swampy woods as well. To fishermen, there is no more scenic, or productive, river than the swampy Ogeechee, which flows 250 miles from the lower Piedmont area of Georgia to the marsh flats of the Atlantic Ocean.

If the Savannah River is known for its commercial success, then the Ogeechee is known for its lack of it. The latter remains one of the most pristine rivers in North America, a murky paradise where rope swings, water moccasins, and fish fries are about the only cause for excitement. The water typically is black, stained by tannic acid from tree roots in the swamps, turning reddish along its journey through middle Georgia's red clay, and eventually becoming blue-green and brackish where the Ogeechee meets the ocean.

King's Ferry in Chatham County is a spot on the river where people gather on weekends and holidays for sun, hot dogs, and diving from an untraveled bridge. Aside from recreation, the Ogeechee provides a livelihood for fishermen, who traditionally guard their secrets for catching the river's prized catfish and Ogeechee shad, a delicacy available each year only from January through March.

BARRIER ISLANDS AND MARSH

The Spanish called this area Guale (pronounced "wallie"), possibly after the chief of the Indians who lived along the chain of golden islands: Tybee, Wassaw, Ossabaw, St. Catherine's, Blackbeard, Sapelo, St. Simons, Jekyll, and Cumberland.

The islands are significant for several reasons. Located on the Atlantic Flyway, they are important to migrating waterfowl, as well as to birds and animals—many endangered—which inhabit the area.

And, as the name implies, the barrier islands serve as protection from nature's fury. Their sandy beaches offer enough resistance to dissipate the tremendous energy of coastal storms, providing a barrier for people and property on the mainland.

Most importantly, behind the barrier islands lie stretches of quiet marsh. Without protection, tidal creeks and salt marshes would cease to be the gentle, nurturing nurseries for so many species of marine life.

The marshes, according to scientists, are the richest acreage on the planet, and Georgia has more than any other state on the Atlantic coast—701,000 acres of salt marshes, mud flats, and swamps. Indeed, the word "Savannah" is a variation of the spelling of "savanna," or grassland.

The perpetual flooding of the marsh by high tides is also the basis for an ecological web that begins with decaying marsh grass and ends with sea creatures that feed each other as well as human beings.

Charles Samz, a retired geophysicist and self-styled naturalist, tells tour groups the story of the fiddler crab—no bigger than a pecan but nonetheless crucial to the fusing of plant and marine life: "When the marsh grass, an annual, dies and decays, the fiddler gathers nutrients by scraping bits of organic matter from the rich mud, spitting out round balls of unused sand in the process. The fiddler, in turn, feeds the fish, crab, and shrimp developing in the tidal creeks. We humans, then, gratefully feast on the seafood that the fiddler has nourished."

The fiddler, truly, is vital to life on the Georgia coast—like a great number of small, but important, things.

The swaying sea oats on Tybee Island are actually a natural form of beach preservation. As the sea oats spread their roots deep into the sand, they anchor the dunes, helping to prevent erosion.

JOSEPH SHIELDS

A Brief History

James Edward Oglethorpe, Savannah's founding father, arrived from England with 35 families on February 12, 1733, to colonize Georgia in the name of King George II.

These were not, of course, the area's first inhabitants. Archaeologists believe that man has lived on the Georgia coast for at least 12,000 years. It is held that nomadic hunters and gatherers of the Southeast stalked the Ice Age mammoth, mastodon, giant bison, and ground sloth, as well as small mammals.

About 4,500 years ago, Archaic Indians populated the area, and archaeologists believe they may have developed the first pottery in North America. The Indians located villages close to tidal creeks, which provided them with plenty of food to eat, particularly oysters. Their discarded oyster shells were piled into heaps, and these shell middens have supplied us with useful information about Indian living habits, diet, and tools. Archaeologists and students continue to dig in a shell midden on Skidaway Island even today, discovering, for example, that Georgia's state shell—the knobble whelk—was a vital ancient digging tool.

The middens provided early colonists with the basis for a primitive building material—tabby. Oyster shells were cooked over a hot fire, then crushed into powder and mixed with sand and water, with whole oyster shells added for binding. Tabby, used to pave sidewalks and construct houses and retaining walls, is still popular with Savannahians today.

The Spaniards also had a presence here: They erected a garrison in 1566 on nearby St. Catherine's Island as defense against the French, but were eventually driven into Florida by the Indians.

In the 1700s, James Edward Oglethorpe had interested 20 Trustees in a colony called Georgia, to be founded on a three-fold purpose: to relieve the distress of the unemployed and persecuted, to enlarge British possessions and extend trade, and to protect English colonies from the Spaniards in Florida, the French in Louisiana, and the native Indians. Colonists were to plant 100 white mulberry trees on every 10 acres of land, in hopes of exporting silk, an enterprise that failed.

Oglethorpe, who would survive a court martial in England and go on to become a general in 1765, was only 36 when he set sail from England in November, 1732. The *Anne*, a 200-ton galley loaded with 120-odd settlers, provisions, and beer, arrived in February 1733, and the weary settlers pitched tents on the top of a steep, sandy bluff beside the Savannah River. Nearby, Oglethorpe found a trading post run by John and Mary Musgrove, who became vital interpreters with the Creek Indians encamped at Yamacraw Village.

"Upon the river-side in the centre of this plain I have laid out the town ... I marked out the town and common; half of the former is already cleared, and the first house was begun yesterday in the afternoon," wrote Oglethorpe to the Trustees almost immediately upon landing.

Oglethorpe was befriended by Tomochichi, chief of the Yamacraws, who obtained permission from other Indians in the area for the English to settle the land between the Savannah and the Altamaha rivers. In his old age, Tomochichi, his wife Senauki, and nephew Toonahowi were rewarded for their generosity with a trip to England, where they were presented by Oglethorpe to the Trustees, to the Archbishop of Canterbury, and to King George II and Queen Caroline. It is very likely that without the aid of the Yamacraws—Tomochichi in particular—Georgia's first settlers would never have survived. Tomochichi was buried in Wright Square in 1737 in an English-Indian ceremony.

Unfortunately, the Indians as a whole were not treated with equal consideration. By 1838, almost all of the Indians were gone from Georgia. Some died of diseases brought by the colonists. Some were killed in battles with the settlers. The remaining Native Americans were forced by federal law to move west of the Mississippi River.

Slaves from South Carolina were also important to the settlement of the new colony. Although slaves were originally banned in Georgia, the governor of South Carolina loaned blacks as day laborers—very likely immediately after the settlers arrived—to run the sawmills to build Savannah's first houses and to teach the colonists this necessary skill.

Savannah gradually grew with the influx of freedom-seeking immigrants from various countries, resulting in a cosmopolitan mix of English, Scots, French, Salzburger, German, and Swiss peoples. But the city did not immediately flourish. At the end of the 18th century, it was still a struggling village of only a few thousand residents.

But that was soon to change.

In 1793, Eli Whitney devised the first commercial cotton gin on Mulberry Plantation, about 10 miles northwest of Savannah.

Although cotton had been shipped from Savannah as early as 1764 by the traders Habersham and Harris, separating the white down from the prickly cotton seed pod remained a slow, laborious task. Whitney's development revolutionized the cotton industry, resulting in a class of wealthy cotton merchants and plantation owners who depended on slave labor. The gin's economic significance is illustrated by these statistics: In 1794, Savannah's exports were less than $500,000. By 1818, exports exceeded $14 million. Likewise, the population increased with the booming cotton business. In 1794, only 2,500 people lived in the city; by 1860, Savannah's population had mushroomed to 22,000. Cotton dominated commerce, culture, and conversation.

The laws banning slaves in Georgia were relaxed in 1751, and by 1771, there were 13,000 slaves in the state, a fact that greatly influenced the culture of the area. Slaves from Sierra Leone in West Africa brought with them their African Gullah customs, stories, and songs. The Gullah heritage still exists up and down the Georgia coast, particularly on the islands of Sapelo and Daufuski, S.C. The Beach Institute, an African-American history and cultural center in Savannah, documents this important link between continents today.

When freedom came after the Civil War, blacks acquired the right to vote and participate in political affairs. Indeed, blacks were elected to the Georgia state legislature as early as 1868. But their political power was short-lived when Northern troops left the South, and Southern whites regained dominance. Many blacks, once promised 40 acres of land and a mule, had to settle for becoming sharecroppers on borrowed land. It would be many years before true equality would seem possible.

As Savannah's importance as a port grew, an event that affected maritime history occurred in 1819, when Moses Rogers served as captain and chief engineer of the *S.S. Savannah,* the first steamship to cross the Atlantic Ocean, sailing from Savannah to Liverpool—an event still celebrated on May 22 as National Maritime Day.

Steamships heralded Savannah's heyday as a port city in the years immediately prior to the Civil War, when ships and steamers were lined up in the river and cotton bales were stacked alongside the busy wharf. Ships, groaning with nature's bounty, were heading up and down the East coast and on to England. The Central of Georgia Railroad, built between 1833 and 1843, linked Savannah's port with cotton fields as far away as Macon, some 150 miles.

New wealth brought with it a society that desired the finer things in life. In the early 1800s, a golf club, jockey club, library society, and dancing academy were formed. Balls were held frequently, and dinner parties were long and elaborate affairs. Because Savannah was an active port city, its citizens seemed more worldly—more British—than many of the other colonists.

The Civil War brought drastic changes.

In 1862, when nearby Fort Pulaski fell to Union troops, Savannah was blockaded. River activity ceased, and the city became eerily quiet. In May 1864, Union General William Tecumseh Sherman, with 62,000 men, 35,000 mules, horses, and cattle, and 2,500 wagons began his infamous march from Atlanta to Savannah, destroying a path 300 miles long and 30 miles wide. On December 21, 1864, Sherman's troops entered Savannah, which, perhaps wisely, gave up without a fight.

Sherman did not burn Savannah. Instead, he sent this telegram to President Lincoln: "I beg to present you as a Christmas-gift the City of Savannah, with one hundred and fifty heavy guns and plenty of ammunition, also about twenty-five thousands bales of cotton." Sherman set up headquarters in the Green-Meldrim House, and his troops camped all over the city, enjoying a pleasant stay, according to diaries.

The end of the war brought the end of the blockade, and by 1867, the port of Savannah was again teaming with ships. Factor's Walk bustled with activity once more. By 1888, the port was at its peak, shipping 2 million bales of cotton yearly on nearly 2,000 vessels.

But Savannah's economic tide began to turn at the end of the century. Although cotton production was up, prices were down. Profits were reinvested in more land and improvements, leaving planters deeper and deeper in debt and the rest of the economy undevel-

New wealth brought with it a society that desired the finer things in life. In the early 1800s, a golf club, jockey club, library society, and dancing academy were formed. Balls were held frequently, and dinner parties were long and elaborate affairs.

James Edward Oglethorpe, an experienced soldier and member of parliament, brought a small group of poor English citizens across the Atlantic in 1733 to settle Georgia's first British colony, Savannah. Oglethorpe spent 10 years building the colony before returning to England in 1743.

oped. The pernicious boll weevil finally put an end to Savannah's teetering cotton empire. The insect reached Georgia in 1915, cutting cotton production by two-thirds. The Savannah economy spiraled and finally collapsed.

Ironically, this may partly have been the city's salvation.

Much of Savannah languished, decaying slowly, while other more prosperous cities were busy tearing down old buildings to build modern ones. Not that Savannah was immune to poor judgment. Historic structures were destroyed and replaced with parking garages and gas stations. Some buildings were demolished for their bricks and lumber alone.

Several events breathed new life into what had become a city that had lost its direction.

In 1917, the Savannah Sugar Refinery, now Savannah Foods and Industries, began operations in the city, and 20 years later, Union Bag, now Union Camp, a kraft paper bag manufacturing company, built a factory here. These two companies offered Savannah an economic base in manufacturing and provided new products to be shipped through Savannah's port.

Manufacturing got another boost in the 1940s, when Savannahians, primarily females, built 88 of the Navy's more than 2,400 Liberty Ships. The cargo ships, nicknamed "Ugly Ducklings," were used to ferry cargo and soldiers during World War II and in the Vietnam War, but were dry docked or scrapped in the 1960s and 1970s by the Navy.

Savannah's reputation as a producer of quality goods was taken to new technological heights in 1978, when Allen E. Paulson purchased Grumman Aircraft. He changed the name to Gulfstream Aerospace Corporation and began producing the world's fastest corporate jet.

Manufacturing of all kinds, from paint to trailers, now makes up 40 percent of Savannah's economy.

On an entirely different front, a group of ladies almost single-handedly spawned Savannah's historic revival. In 1954, the City Market, an open-air market that sold everything from freshly killed chickens to produce, was destroyed to make way for a parking garage. Next on the demolition list was the Isaiah Davenport house, a Federal style home built in 1820. A handful of friends, led by artist Anna Hunter, formed Historic Savannah Foundation, saved the house, and spurred a restoration movement that has not only led to civic pride, but also has attracted untold numbers of tourists. Tourism is now the fastest-growing segment of the Savannah economy.

Savannah's history is rich with colorful characters who have made their contributions to religion, art, music, law, maritime trade, industry, business, banking, the media, and medicine.

One of the most flamboyant and influential of them all was Juliette Gordon Low, called "Daisy" by her family and friends. Daisy was born in 1860 to Eleanor Kinzie, a high-spirited Yankee who was said to slide down banisters and swear, and William Washington Gordon II, a cotton trader whose father had built the Central of Georgia Railroad.

As a girl, Daisy was a stubborn tomboy, a rascal. She grew to be a lovable eccentric who studied palmistry, wore real vegetables on her hats, and went trout fishing with Rudyard Kipling wearing full evening dress. She was almost deaf in one year from insisting that a doctor treat an earache with silver nitrate. At her wedding to William Mackay Low in 1886, a grain of rice lodged in her good ear, tragically leaving her deaf in that ear as well.

Following an unhappy marriage and the death of her husband, Juliette Low shuttled between Savannah, England, and Scotland, feeling aimless. Then, at the age of 50, she met Gen. Sir Robert Baden-Powell, a British military hero and organizer of the Boy Scouts and the Girl Guides. He gave Juliette the idea of forming a similar program for American girls.

On March 12, 1912, in Savannah, Juliette Gordon Low formed the first two patrols of the Girl Guides—later to become the Girl Scouts—spawning a movement that has influenced the lives of more than 50 million women.

Juliette Low's Girl Guide handbook, written in 1913, was a new vision of what women's lives could be, providing useful information on subjects like first aid, domestic arts, gardening, astronomy, and ecology—not usual topics for women of the time.

"The numbers of women who have taken up aviation prove that women's nerves are good enough for flying," she wrote. "... and now it is within the power of any girl with perseverance and close study to enter the medical profession, and even to rise up to distinction as a doctor and to honorable celebrity."

Her birthplace, a Regency townhouse built in 1818-21 at the corner of Oglethorpe Avenue and Bull Street, has been restored to the late 1800s period when Juliette would have been living there and features many

"Change in Savannah is something that has to be measured and considered a little longer than in most places. But Savannah is not resistant to change."

original family furnishings. Maintained by the Girl Scouts as a museum and national program center, the home has welcomed more than 1 million visitors since 1956, when it was one of the first homes in the city to be restored. Tour guides delight visitors with stories of Daisy Low, the amazing woman who, for the last days of her life, was never seen out of her Girl Scout uniform—a campaign hat on her head and a whistle and tin cup at her waist. She is buried in Laurel Grove Cemetery in Savannah.

Savannah's history is rich with colorful characters who have made their contributions to religion, art, music, law, maritime trade, industry, business, banking, the media, and medicine.

Savannahians are equally proud of native son Johnny Mercer, who won Academy Awards for "Moon River," theme of the 1962 film *Breakfast at Tiffany's* and for "Days of Wine and Roses," theme song for the 1963 movie of the same name. Hundreds of others, like "Jeepers, Creepers," and "Autumn Leaves," cause Mercer, who died in 1976 and is buried in Bonaventure Cemetery, to be considered one of American's most beloved lyricists.

The city also provided inspiration to James Pierpont, who wrote "Jingle Bells," and to writers Flannery O'Connor and Conrad Aiken. Actors Miriam Hopkins, Charles Coburn, Diana Scarwid, and Stacy Keach have roots here as well.

Although there have been any number of philanthropists in Savannah, none have been quite so quietly generous as the late Mills B. Lane Jr., son of the founder of the C&S banking system, now part of the NationsBank chain. Lane, a tireless advocate of Savannah's restoration movement, is credited with renovations to downtown squares, the development of River Street's Waving Girl Park, and the donation of 250 acres on Savannah's south side for the campus of Armstrong State College. His most glittering legacy was the $240,000 gilding of the dome and cupola on City Hall in 1987, funded by the Ships of the Sea Museum, a maritime museum which Lane founded. Lane always shunned publicity, saying, "I could have done a lot

more." He died in 1989, and now rests in Bonaventure Cemetery.

Modern history will surely include the name of W.W. Law, a retired postal clerk who has spent a lifetime researching African-American history and promoting black pride. His efforts have been rewarded with the establishment of the centers he runs: the King-Tisdell Cottage, a black history museum; and the Beach Institute, an African-American cultural center, both located downtown in the Beach Institute Historic Neighborhood, one of the city's oldest black neighborhoods. Law, who in May 1992, was a recipient of a Governor's Awards in the Humanities, lives up to this passage he has read to museum visitors from Janie Hunter's book, *Ain't You Got a Right to the Tree of Life: The People of St. Johns Island, S.C.*: "What I know, I try to teach the children. That is the black tradition, so the generation can go on and won't die out."

In 1991, a new name was added to Savannah's list of distinguished citizens when Clarence Thomas, a black lawyer who was head of the Equal Employment Opportunity Commission, survived controversial confirmation hearings and was appointed to the U.S. Supreme Court. Thomas was born in Pin Point, a rural community outside Savannah. After a fire destroyed his home, his family split up, and Thomas went to live with his grandparents on 32nd Street in inner-city Savannah. He attended Catholic schools taught by Franciscan nuns.

Standing beside President George Bush on the day of his nomination in July 1991, Thomas choked with emotion when he remembered the influence of his Savannah roots, the grandparents who encouraged him, and the nuns who educated him. He said he hoped, if confirmed, "to be an example to those who are where I was and to show them that, indeed, there is hope."

Hope is something most Savannahians—whose history includes fires, hurricanes, yellow fever epidemics, and financial ruin—believe in. And it is the belief in good things to come that propels them into the future.

Blacks have been vital to the success of Savannah since the city's first days. Although slaves were originally banned in the Georgia colony, they were brought over from South Carolina to tcach Savannah settlers to run the sawmills. African-American historic and cultural contributions are displayed at the King-Tisdell Cottage at 514 East Huntingdon Street.

The Savannah Character

There was a time, not very long ago, when it was possible to give a fairly accurate description of the Savannah character because so many of the people who lived here had been here all their lives. Even today, particularly among a group who can claim to have been "bo-wan he-ah," there is a special speech, an eccentricity, a unique Savannah spirit that is still identifiable.

But Savannah is full of new blood from other parts of the country and from other countries as well. And so, the lines are a little blurry when you begin to talk of what a Savannahian is and isn't.

Savannah is still a place where women often have two first names, like Martha Elizabeth and Sarah Kate. It's a place where an executive might be called Buddy or Chip. Like the rest of the South, Savannah tends to favor nicknames, perhaps because we'd rather do our banking with someone we've called Trey since childhood than with someone we don't know at all.

Names can be important in Savannah—too important, complain some—and the first few minutes getting acquainted are typically spent trying to establish just what sort of name you have and whether or not you can be connected with anyone—or anything—significant. How you earn your money, where you live, where your children go to school, your church affiliation, and whether your game is golf, tennis, or bridge will come later. The name check comes first.

Being a native Savannahian is something to brag about, and the deeper the roots go, the more bragging rights you have. Yet, particularly with the success of The Landings community on Skidaway Island, natives have been joined by a large number of transplants bringing with them a wealth of new ideas, talents, and energy—and the desire to assimilate.

The newcomers find, with some consternation, that they have to be patient while waiting to be regarded as true Savannahians.

"A Savannahian, by tradition, is someone who has lived here a considerable length of time, not necessarily a native, but someone who knows the place well," suggests Arthur Gordon, author and former magazine editor who was born in Savannah and has come back to enjoy a working retirement. Gordon undoubtedly qualifies as a Savannahian—his family has been in the city since 1790, and he was a favorite nephew of Girl Scouts founder Juliette Gordon Low.

Gordon has known several generations of Savannahians and today watches the activities of the city's movers and shakers with fond irritation. He expounds on some of our historic peculiarities:

"We tend to be traditionalists and are suspicious that the past may have been better than the present, and that tends to affect our reactions to things.

"We mostly have good manners and tend to value them more than other people do. For generations, it was more important to have good manners than money, because there wasn't any money to be had.

"We tend to have a contentious streak: Whatever change is proposed, somebody will leap up to oppose it. That's not too good for progress. And we don't seem to have the drive they have in some other towns.

"We are good storytellers, great raconteurs. We have a droll sense of humor. You go to dinner parties, and you may as well be at the theater.

"We are a proud people, and we have a lot to be proud of. But we occasionally take offense too easily.

"I view Savannahians, on the whole, with great affection, and, at times, great exasperation."

Dennis Smith, vice president of sales for Carson Products, a manufacturer of ethnic beauty supplies, has moved 13 times and has spent four years in Savannah. People here, he says, are particularly friendly: "We will talk to you and find out whether you are visiting and where you are visiting from. And then we will begin to brag on our city.

"People seem to have time here—time to stop on the side of the road and help you change a flat tire and time to come get you when your car breaks down. In a bigger city, there is no time, except to complain. We live at a slower pace here, but people seem to put themselves in your shoes and that makes them respond differently to you."

Dr. Annette Brock, a native Savannahian who graduated from Savannah State College and is now its acting president, says the city's past is the glue that holds all Savannahians together:

"A Savannahian is really a person who embraces Savannah's history, Savannah's problems, and Savannah's progress, and feels inextricably bound to its future. Savannahians understand that theirs is not a perfect city, but it is a good place, and they want to see it prosper and grow. They have no desire to go anyplace else.

"Savannah is a friendly place. There is room in Savannah for all people who are here, all the diverse groups. It's part of our character."

Those diverse citizens, according to 1990 census figures, include 64,131 Caucasians and 69,890 minority citizens within the city limits, a fact that affects, among other things, the political makeup of the eight-member City Council, which includes four African-Americans. In 1991, Alderman Floyd Adams won an at-large seat, marking the first time a black has won a citywide election. The same year, Republican Susan Weiner, a former New Yorker, defied the odds to beat the charismatic, 21-year incumbent, Democrat John Rousakis, to become the city's first female mayor.

The largest number of Savannah's minority residents are African-American, but there are a fair number of people who claim Asian, Japanese, Chinese, Korean, and American Indian heritages. In Chatham County, which includes Savannah and the surrounding island communities, there are 218,000 residents—131,000 Caucasians, 83,000 African-Americans, and 4,000 other minorities. Throw in surrounding counties—Bryan, Effingham, Liberty, Beaufort (SC), Jasper (SC), Hampton (SC), Screven, Evans, Bulloch and McIntosh—and the census number swells to 500,000, significant because these counties look to Savannah as a primary employer, as well as for medical care, shopping, and entertainment.

"We are really a melting pot of peoples, with many nationalities and ethnic groups," explains Arthur A. "Don" Mendonsa, who has watched Savannah develop during the 27 years he has served as city manager.

As has always been the case in Savannah, there are families of prosperity and poverty. Twenty percent of the area's citizens earn less than $10,000, and more than 16 percent earn more than $50,000 annually.

Savannah faces its share of urban problems: crime, drugs, homelessness, unemployment, teenage pregnancy, illiteracy, and AIDS top the list.

"We have old South and new South. We have old wealth and new wealth. But we also realize as a city that our poorest citizens have critical needs that must be addressed," Mendonsa says. "Slowly but surely—at a glacier's pace it seems like sometimes—we are beginning to address those needs.

"The community is changing," Mendonsa asserts, "and one big change is that African-Americans are more and more moving into political leadership. At the same time, the city has been successful in maintaining racial harmony."

Outsiders, in fact, often comment on the lack of racial tension in Savannah. That may be, Arthur Gordon muses, because blacks and whites have been culturally bound from the beginning of Savannah's history:

"We have a legacy of tolerance and affection because we grew up together. In the days of confrontation, during the Civil Rights movement, our negotiations were handled successfully because we spoke the same language. We knew each other, understood each other."

Dr. Brock sees race relations a little differently: "Savannah, more than any other place in the South, seems to have found a way to approach solutions to its problems through peaceful means. When other Southern cities had periods of violence, Savannah's citizens put Savannah first, put the city above all other factors, and came together, not as quickly as some would like, but slowly.

"Change in Savannah is something that has to be measured and considered a little longer than most places," Dr. Brock adds. "But Savannah is not resistant to change."

Savannah is full of new blood from other parts of the country and from other countries as well. And so, the lines are a little blurry when you begin to talk of what a Savannahian is and isn't.

A LOVE OF TRADITION

Regardless of race, religion, or income, one thing all Savannahians seem to share is a love of the land and water. We are fishermen, boaters, shrimpers, crabbers, and hunters. Savannah is a place where, during the sweltering summer, it is acceptable for men to show up for relaxed island church services in khakis, knit shirts, and deck shoes so they won't have to change before heading out to the docks.

What *is* important in Savannah is that you do show up for church. Savannahians are historically bound to their religious roots. John Wesley, the father of Methodism, preached at Christ Church in Savannah and is said to have begun the first Protestant Sunday school in the nation there. The third Jewish congrega-

Forsyth Park was the brainchild of William Hodgson, who convinced the city council in 1851 to set aside 10 acres of pine forest, which he enclosed at his own expense to keep out the cattle. Today, the park's 31 acres of manicured beauty provide a setting for walking, frisbee-throwing, soccer, football, and tennis, as well as a variety of festivals and cultural events. The cast-iron fountain in Forsyth Park was erected in 1858 and renovated in 1988 through a community-wide effort.

▼ JOSEPH BYRD

26

tion in America was organized here in 1733, and its members completed the Gothic style Mickve Israel Temple in 1878. Both the First African Baptist Church and the First Bryan Baptist Church were organized in the late 1700s as two of the oldest black congregations in the United States.

Many families today travel from some faraway suburb to attend services downtown in the same historic church as their mothers and fathers did, preferably sitting on the same pew. Leave tradition for a more convenient location? Savannahians are too loyal for that.

"The church in the black community plays a very specific role in social as well as political and spiritual life," says The Rev. Mathew Southall Brown, pastor for 22 years at St. John Baptist Church. "Most people in the black community look upon the church as the organization that provides leadership."

Savannahians love to entertain, usually informally. But occasionally, they bring out the family china, silver, and linen in a style reminiscent of old times. A classic Savannah dinner party, which might begin with cold crab legs and jumbo boiled shrimp as appetizers, move on to shad stuffed with roe, and conclude with Savannah trifle and coffee with benne seed cookies, is an event to be relished. Just as popular is the mid-winter oyster roast, where Savannahians don blue jeans and winter coats and stand around a table heaped with smoked oysters that have just been shoveled from a burlap-covered piece of tin positioned over a roaring fire. An oyster knife, a glove on the left hand to avoid puncturing the meaty flesh of your hand while opening the oysters, melted butter, saltines, and beer are the only required oyster-roast accompaniments.

"Our dining is governed by the seasons. We have mild winters, but we have hot, hot summers and so we eat light accordingly. We eat outdoors in the fall and spring, when it is so beautiful," explains Elizabeth Terry, who has become something of a food historian and whose culinary talents at her restaurant, Elizabeth on 37th, have led to her selection by *Food and Wine* magazine as one of the top 25 restaurants in the United States.

"Savannahians have a long tradition of eating *with* people, and the oyster roast and the crab boil continue in this vein. In some parts of the country, people have given up on dining with friends, but I think they will miss the experience, and eventually return to it. Savannahians never will have to get back to it, because it's a part of life we have never given up."

When not on the water, in church, or dining with friends, Savannahians are apt to be outdoors, taking advantage of the myriad of activities that can be enjoyed almost 12 months of the year.

The huge parks—Forsyth in downtown, Daffin in midtown and Lake Mayer on the southside—are typically jammed with picnickers, runners and tennis players. Daffin also attracts fans to Grayson Stadium, home of the Savannah Cardinals, the city's Class A minor league baseball team. The modern Allen E. Paulson softball complex, funded by its namesake, contains five well-maintained softball fields.

There are 32 supervised playgrounds in the city. More than 1,500 children play baseball on more than 100 teams, and about 2,700 adults play softball on city leagues. Youth soccer attracts 1,300 participants, and thousands of Savannahians play team tennis. There are 20 golf courses in a 50-mile radius, as well as 16 marinas, 10 charter/deep sea boating services, and two sail harbor services, all of which are kept busy at least nine months of the year.

Outdoor festivals are a natural way for Savannahians to celebrate, and such festivals are held in grand style and with great frequency: the Greek Festival, the Scottish Games and Highlands Gathering, Oktoberfest, the Savannah Arts Festival, the Black Arts Festival, the Great Atlantic Seafood Festival, the Jewish Food Festival, Night in Old Savannah, the Savannah Jazz Festival, Georgia Day, the Festival of Trees, Savannah On Stage!, and the Savannah Folk Music Festival, to name a few.

The St. Patrick's Day parade, which attracts an estimated 300,000 outsiders, is one of the largest in the United States. Waterfront festivals alone bring about 450,000 people yearly to Historic Savannah. During the Christmas holidays, downtown Savannah is transformed into a magical place of lights, carriage tours, and all-natural decorations in the squares. The spring Tour of Homes brings visitors from around the country to view private residences and "ooh" and "ahh" over the azaleas in full bloom.

Excitement is also brewing over the pre-Olympic regattas that will be hosted in Savannah in 1993, 1994 and 1995. And in September of 1992, a Maritime Festival was held to celebrate Savannah's nautical heritage, as well as to promote Olympic fever.

Many Savannahians enjoy a quality of life unmatched elsewhere, but they are also uniquely touched by those who are less fortunate. Savannahians are caring and generous, a people with heart.

THE VOLUNTEER SPIRIT

Many Savannahians enjoy a quality of life un-matched elsewhere, but they are also uniquely touched by those who are less fortunate. Savannahians are caring and generous, a people with heart.

Residents of The Landings at Skidaway are often cited for their important volunteer contributions to diverse groups ranging from the homeless, disadvantaged youth, and battered women to the museums and symphony. Landings residents are currently building three Habitat for Humanity homes that will be deeded to low-income residents.

Hazel Brown, one of almost 600 Skidaway residents registered as volunteers with United Way, explains it this way: "Many of us come here to retire, and we never had the opportunity to volunteer before. At first, we feel we have a debt to pay. After that, it comes from the heart."

"Our programs live and die with volunteers," says Joe Shearouse, director of Leisure Services for the city. "All of our youth programs are coached by volunteers. The city pays for umpires and manages the fields, but we could never hire enough coaches."

Rotary Club members provided lighted fountains for Daffin Park and are currently raising money to install antique lighting around the park. Individuals led the effort to refurbish the Forsyth Fountain and to build the Vietnam Veterans Memorial in Emmett Park. The Junior League of Savannah has, since 1927, given $873,000 to jump-start programs that range from historic preservation and recycling to Girl Scouting in the inner city. United Way raised $5.5 million in Chatham County in 1991, and Savannah leads Georgia in per capita giving to United Way.

"I think one of Savannah's strengths is the large number of people who are willing to make a difference in the lives of others," explains Bill Daniel, chairman of the Chamber of Commerce as well as his church's administrative board. "I think it's a direct result of the religious commitment of the community, not in a traditional, organized sense, but as an important part of our way of life down here."

▶ JOHN CARRINGTON, *SAVANNAH NEWS-PRESS*

Policemen in downtown Savannah use innovative approaches—bicycle and horse patrols, as well as foot patrols—to be more accessible to the people they serve and protect.

A Diverse Economy

When it comes to making money, this is a city of contrasts. Savannah is considered provincial, yet it produces an aeronautical masterpiece, the Gulfstream jet. It has a reputation for being "sleepy," but has aggressively prepared itself for the 21st century. Its past has been preserved, protected and promoted, yet leaders know that only by looking ahead to new enterprise can Savannah realize her true potential.

Savannahians are able to make a living today the way residents historically have done so, as soldiers and shippers. But the city learned a valuable lesson following the collapse of the cotton empire: Diversity is the key to a healthy economy. Today, Savannah's economy has expanded into five broad areas: manufacturing, the military, the port, service industries, and tourism.

Savannah was established by the English primarily for colonial defense; today, 22,000 soldiers trained for rapid deployment at Hunter Army Airfield in Savannah and Ft. Stewart in nearby Hinesville still pursue the long-standing tradition of defending their country.

The military accounts for a remarkable 20 percent of the area's income with a payroll in 1990 close to $475 million and expenditures in the area topping $166 million. In addition to the 22,000 soldiers in Coastal Georgia, the combined posts of Hunter and Ft. Stewart support almost 100,000 family members and military retirees, who look to the bases for commissary, administrative, and medical support.

Savannahians are justly proud of their soldiers, members of the 24th Infantry Division, for Coastal Georgia armed forces are the first to fight in any conflict. They were first to arrive in Saudi Arabia during Operation Desert Storm and were the division that led the deep attack into Iraq during the 100-hour ground war. In addition, Savannah is home to the special operations units, including the 1st Ranger Battalion, which took part in the invasion of Granada and the Panama liberation.

But the relationship between Savannah and the military runs deeper than numbers and statistics.

Maj. Gen. Barry R. McCaffrey, commanding general in 1992 of the division as well as both Ft. Stewart and Hunter, says life along the Georgia coast is something of a prize: "The soldiers could not enjoy a better place to live and work. On a day-to-day basis, you can sense a great working relationship between the military and civilian communities founded on concerned local leadership, trust, and mutual respect. This 'teamwork' is not new. It is a fact that the soldiers of the 24th Infantry Division have long found an assignment to this area to be personally and professionally rewarding. The people of Georgia have always treated the military well."

Savannah, almost immediately after its founding, became established as a port city. That tradition continues, and the port and related distribution industries account for another 20 percent of the city's income. In container volume, the port of Savannah ranks 12th in the nation. More than 7,000 people are employed locally in port-related jobs. International trade through Georgia's ports provides 63,000 jobs throughout the state, generating more than $189 million in state and local taxes and U.S. Customs collections of more than $200 million per year.

A soaring new bridge, which spans the Savannah River 185 feet high, can accommodate 98 percent of the world's shipping fleet. Road and rail systems connect Savannah to Atlanta, the premier distribution center in the South. The port is the point of entry for a surprising variety of products, including melons, bananas and pineapples from the tropics and wine from South Africa. Kaolin clay—a fine, white clay used to make porcelain and as a filler in textiles, paper, and rubber—is one of the largest volume commodities shipped. Others include steel, forest products, machinery, granite, copper, jet fuels, liquor, and latex.

Thanks to the cotton industry, cotton seed oil had been refined at the Southern Cotton Oil Company since 1885. However, in 1899, Dr. David Wesson discovered a process of making lighter, blander products from soybeans that led to the manufacturing of Wesson Oil and Snowdrift brand solid shortening. Today, 150 million pounds of vegetable oils and shortenings are manufactured in Savannah at the Hunt-Wesson refineries, one of only two Wesson oil refineries in the world. (The other is in Memphis, Tennessee.) Wesson products are transported by rail, truck, and ship throughout the United States and to other countries under other labels as well.

Aside from oil production, however, Savannah in the 1900s was in an economic slump. Then two companies moved in and expanded Savannah's potential to make money in manufacturing.

In 1917, cousins Richard H. Sprague of San Francisco and Benjamin Alexander Oxnard of New Orleans opened a sugar refinery in Port Wentworth, a few miles from Savannah. A site on the Savannah River was chosen because of accessibility to the port for receiving raw sugar and the availability of the rail line for distributing sugar to markets. Savannah Foods, which is still run by members of the Sprague and Oxnard families, continues to operate the Savannah refinery as its flagship facility, but now has eight more operations in locations throughout the country. The company employs more than 700 people and ships Dixie Crystals sugar throughout the world.

In 1935, Union Bag Company, now Union Camp, built a factory in the city because of accessibility to vast forests of Southern pines. The trees were made into paper using a process developed by Dr. Charles Herty, a Savannah chemist. The paper plant was small, and there were weeks when C&S banker Mills B. Lane had to ensure that the company could make the payroll. The bank's faith in Union Camp paid off. The company is now the world's largest kraft paper mill and one of Chatham County's largest manufacturing employers, with 3,200 workers.

"Manufacturing gave Savannah a new way to make money, a leap of economic energy," explains John Hicks, vice president for business development with the Savannah Area Chamber of Commerce.

Today, manufacturing accounts for about 40 percent of the area's payroll. Savannah manufacturers use by-products from the paper industry to produce a variety of chemicals, Great Dane truck trailers are manufactured here, and fiberglass naval mine hunters are built at Intermarine USA. Carson Products is one of the largest ethnic beauty supply producers in the country. A relative newcomer on the scene is the Ft. Howard Paper Company in Effingham County, which produces paper items totally from recyclable materials.

In 1978 entrepreneur Allen E. Paulson moved here and purchased Grumman Aircraft, now Gulfstream Aerospace Corporation. Paulson began producing what

has become the world's fastest and finest corporate jet, the Gulfstream IV. The company, with about 3,400 employees and a 2-million-square-foot facility, is owned by a partnership of Gulfstream Aerospace and Forstmann Little & Company, a New York investment firm. Paulson, whose personal contributions include major funding for a university stadium in Statesboro and a softball complex in Savannah, remains chairman of the board.

Service industries—banking, health care, insurance, law and accounting—make up another 10 percent of Savannah's economy. Savannah has become a major job generator and a regional retail and service center, which, in turn, has resulted in an expansion in the media, advertising, and retail markets.

Shoppers come from surrounding counties to spend money in Oglethorpe Mall and Savannah Mall. They also come to Savannah for quality health care, an industry that brings in $500 million annually.

There are three major acute-care hospitals in the area—Memorial Medical Center, Candler General Hospital, and St. Joseph's Hospital, each equipped to handle just about any procedure short of organ transplants or treatment of major burns.

"Savannah is able to attract physicians who have graduated from the top medical schools in the country. We have specialists in every field, and the hospitals are able to buy the high-tech equipment that the doctors ask for. All three of the hospitals are well-equipped and have excellent staffs," explains Michael Zoller, M.D., president of the Georgia Medical Society, representing 450 physicians in Chatham, Bryan, and Effingham counties.

Tourism, the fastest-growing segment of the economy, accounts for the final 10 percent of Savannah's income.

"With the restoration of the Historic District and the formation of the Savannah Convention and Visitors Bureau in the 1970s to market the area, Savannah found yet another way to make a living," the Chamber's John Hicks explains.

Quaint, hospitable, historic inns, larger hotels with meeting rooms and convention space, innovative restaurants, tour companies, and cruise ships thrive thanks to

Savannahians are able to make a living today the way residents historically have done so, as soldiers and shippers. But the city learned a valuable lesson following the collapse of the cotton empire: Diversity is the key to a healthy economy.

Savannah has become a major job generator and a regional retail and service center, which, in turn, has resulted in an expansion in the media, advertising, and retail markets.

the tourist market. Tourists also visit museums, attend concerts and performances, and purchase art and antiques. The city accommodates them in 94 hotels and motels, offering 7,000 rooms. In recent years, the number of visitors to Savannah has doubled, and the amount of visitor spending has tripled. In 1991, the tourist trade attracted more than 5 million visitors who spent more than $579 million locally.

Through the Savannah Economic Development Partnership, managed by the Savannah Economic Development Authority, a state-chartered body, the city actively solicits new business. And, for the most part, the city has planned wisely for its future, according to Hicks:

"We have made enormous investments in our infrastructure. The citizens have passed two local option sales taxes that have been used to match state and federal funds to build roads. We are now on our way to having a modern transportation system. We are getting ready to launch into a $40 million wastewater treatment program, and make $36 million worth of drainage improvements.

"Local industries have spent well over a billion dollars in capital improvements and equipment. The Crossroads Business Park, planned by the Savannah Economic Development Authority, has the potential for 13,000 new jobs. We are just embarking on a $73 million airport expansion. The state has just approved a $63 million port improvement package. For a small town, we have expended extraordinary energy in investing in the stuff that really matters. We are uniquely set up to meet the future."

And, because Savannah's eggs are not all in one basket, Hicks believes that the economy is relatively secure: "We never abandoned the old, but we have found new ways of making a living. Some cities are totally dependent on one economic source, which makes them vulnerable to changes in national policy. We are a town of small and diverse enterprises, which buffers us when the economy shifts."

A construction worker is silhouetted against concrete and steel that, in August of 1990, became the Savannah Mall, 139 businesses and more than a million square feet of shopping and dining space.

The Arts and Education

Savannahians are understandably proud of many things about their city, but recently, it seems, the areas of art and education deserve special recognition.

Savannah is really a small city; and, therefore, it seems surprising that so many accomplished artists are drawn here. Perhaps it is the sheer beauty of the place. Or that Savannahians seem hungry for the arts. Or even that the city is willing to pay for the arts.

"The symphony receives strong support from the city of Savannah, and that is quite unusual for a city of this size," explains Philip Greenberg, music director and conductor of the Savannah Symphony. "I've lived in quite a few cities, and it is rare to see the arts given as high a priority by city government as they are in Savannah."

Nor are the arts reserved for those who can afford a $20 ticket. Every year, as many as 5,000 citizens hear the symphony perform free in Forsyth Park. Another 8,000 set up lawn chairs, picnic blankets, and coolers along the Savannah River when the orchestra performs on River Street. The city pays for both concerts, as well as for a number of innovative arrangements that send professional artists out into the community.

Savannah set aside $700,000 in 1992 for the arts, funding supplied partially by a special hotel/motel tax. Much of that was spent to purchase contracts from professional artists and cultural agencies to teach, perform, and give workshops in schools, senior citizen centers, and city parks.

"Our belief is all citizens should be able to fulfill their potential for creative expression," explains Leslie Gordon, who left her job in 1992 as director of cultural affairs for the city to become deputy director of the Cultural Olympiad for the Atlanta Committee for the Olympic Games. "The city believes that the arts are a community service, like fire protection, and that everyone is entitled to receive that service."

This commitment to the arts carries over into the public school system, which currently has four arts-oriented magnet programs—two elementary, one middle school, and one high school. The curriculum includes history, aesthetics, and criticism, in addition to performances and productions. That's because, as explained by Dr. Nancy Hooten, administrative coordinator for the arts programs, this broad approach demands a higher level of thinking skills.

"Arts," she says, "are not the icing on the cake, but a central part of the education of children. When you are talking about multiculturalism or a child's ethnic heritage, you are talking about the arts."

The hope is that, in years to come, children who have been challenged by a serious study of the arts will be well-rounded adults who can appreciate the multitude of talent Savannah has to offer.

That talent is seen in a number of galleries and studios throughout the city, most located in the downtown Historic District and in City Market, a cluster of restored warehouses where a number of artists and craftspersons work full time. The Beach Institute, housed in the oldest black school in the Deep South, has carved out a role to preserve the work and recognize the talent of past and contemporary black artists. Opened in 1990, the institute features historic African art, as well as works of modern black artists.

The Telfair Academy of Arts and Sciences, which functions as the city's major art museum, has a permanent collection of 2,500 works, primarily fine art, collectibles, and furniture created in America and Europe since the Revolutionary War. In addition, The Telfair sponsors changing exhibitions, adult lectures, school tours, family Sundays, and professional consultations for collectors.

The local colony of artists, which is estimated to be in the hundreds, includes not only weavers, iron workers, potters, painters, and illustrators, but also writers, poets, actors, and dancers who follow in the city's abundant arts tradition.

"Savannah has a rich art community," says Floriana Venetico, an art gallery owner who encourages the marketing of Savannah artists nationally. "The local history and beauty nurtures artists, like Paris inspired so many artists and writers. The Savannah College of Art and Design has also expanded the arts by attracting top professors from around the world, not to mention talented students."

Ms. Venetico believes that marketing serious art could become a new way to attract visitors to the city: "A city with a reputation for the arts draws a tourist searching for a certain watercolor or an antique. Our artists are one of our best-kept secrets."

The Savannah Symphony's conductor, Philip Greenberg, is equally high on the city's musicians. "I think the Savannah orchestra is generally recognized as one of the best of any city its size in the country. We have a major, professional orchestra with a $2 million budget. That means that we regularly attract major guest artists in the profession. They do not need to perform in Savannah, Georgia, but they are coming for the quality of the orchestra."

Jazz, too, is currently enjoying a renaissance and attracting a nationwide audience.

"It is as if we have made a great archaeological discovery," says Dr. Julius "Boo" Hornstein, who has studied the evolution of Savannah's jazz history and has promoted its resurgence for 10 years. "The more you dig, the more you find. Many people associated with jazz in Savannah have been performing for 50 years or more and are still going strong. They're as good as they've ever been."

The Coastal Jazz Association has created a vehicle to showcase major talent, The Savannah Jazz Festival, held for one week each September. Musicians of national prominence join local talent, whose nuances have produced what is called the "Savannah sound." Performances take place throughout the city—on River Street, in City Market, in Forsyth Park—and most are free.

Savannah has two full-time theater companies, City Lights and the Savannah Theatre, in addition to drama offerings at the Savannah College of Art and Design, Savannah State College, and Armstrong State College. Ballet South is the city's non-professional dance company, providing an outlet for dancers and training for students, some of whom go on to large professional companies.

Running parallel to the performing and visual arts are the popular decorative and functional arts: antiques, handmade rugs, and other collectibles seen not only in the city's house museums but in private homes when Savannah's mansions are opened to the public during charity tours.

Artist Ann Osteen has worked for years to preserve Savannah's decorative heritage. From peeling paint, she has created a line of earth colors called the Savannah Spectrum—distinctive blues, browns, mauves, and greens—that give a continuity of color to the downtown cityscape. From ceiling rubbings, original wallpapers,

fabrics, china, and rugs, Osteen has catalogued designs that have been translated into wallpapers, fabrics, and rugs known as The Historic Savannah Collection, produced and marketed by the Scalamandre firm.

"People come here specifically to purchase and enjoy the decorative arts," explains Arthur Smith, one of the largest antique dealers in the Southeast. "People see how these collectibles are displayed in the house museums, and you can't imagine the impact that has on the interest in antiques. Savannah is beautiful architecturally, historically and naturally. All of it interrelates."

If there is a single major area about which all Savannah citizens are in agreement, it is education: An educated citizenry means a skilled and employable work force. A working citizenry buys more goods, supports the arts, and, most critical, is better able to stay off welfare rolls.

Yet, in the past, it seemed as if an educated citizenry was out of Savannah's reach. Test scores were low, dropout rates were high. As recent as 1984, only 34 percent of all public school graduates went on to any form of higher education. But Patrick Russo, the new, energetic, positive-thinking superintendent of public schools, says all that is changing for the 34,000 young people he is responsible for educating. (Another 8,000 Chatham County youth attend private schools.)

"In 1990, the number of public school graduates going to some form of higher education rose to 61 percent, and 55 percent of those chose some form of college," Russo says. "A 20 percent increase in less than 10 years is amazing. It shows that we are pushing towards excellence." Public school seniors in 1992 received a remarkable $4.2 million in major scholarships to colleges and universities throughout the nation.

Russo was warned before coming to Savannah in August of 1991 that the public school system was outdated and ineffective.

"My observations since then are that the concerns people had about this system were perceptions and not reality," Russo says. "The average citizen had no idea how good we are. Once people visit our schools, they *know* we've got something good going. What existed 10 or even five years ago in the public schools does not exist today."

Nineteen magnet academies offer elementary, middle, or high school students a chance to develop a

The local colony of artists, which is estimated to be in the hundreds, includes not only weavers, iron workers, potters, painters, and illustrators, but also writers, poets, actors, and dancers who follow in the city's abundant arts tradition.

Young environmentalists have ample opportunity for hands-on learning at the Savannah Science Museum on Paulsen Street.

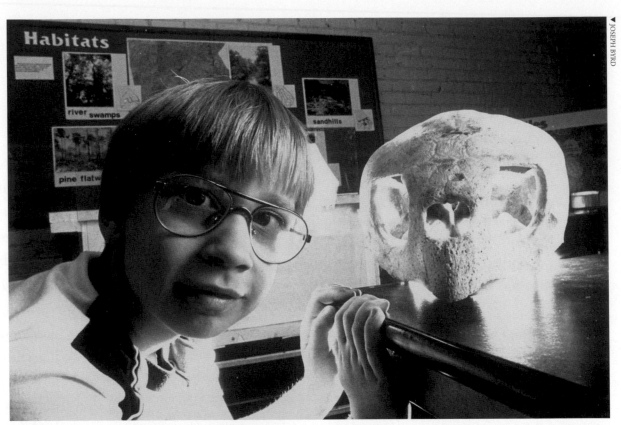

specialized talent or interest. To reach disadvantaged teens and keep them in school, Chatham County applied for and received a five-year, $10 million grant from the Annie E. Casey Foundation, formed by the founders of United Parcel Service to give qualifying cities the chance to improve the lives of at-risk youth. One of five cities to receive the grant, Savannah now serves 1,200 youths and their families in direct case management through the Youth Futures Initiative, and helps thousands more through informal programs aimed at keeping youths in school, reducing teenage pregnancy, improving health, and providing lifeskills training for the future.

Improving education is also a high priority of the business community, since a strong school system is critical when recruiting workers or attracting new business to the area. Members of the Savannah Area Chamber of Commerce and the school system have bonded to form the Savannah Compact, with a common goal of readying students for satisfying work in the Savannah area.

In the area of higher education, three units of the University System of Georgia also serve Coastal Georgia, each with a special niche in the market.

Georgia Southern University in nearby Statesboro, Georgia, the newest university in the state, has 13,000 students enrolled and has the responsibility for graduate-level education in Southeast Georgia.

Armstrong State College, a senior residential college in Savannah, attracts a constituency of 5,000 students, 40 percent of whom are "non-traditional," meaning they are 25 or older. More than a dozen degrees are offered in health professions alone, and it is rare when a graduate in any of Armstrong's health professions doesn't have a job upon graduation.

Savannah State College has 2,700 students, three quarters of whom are African-American. The first institution of higher learning chartered by the state for African-Americans, Savannah State College continues its commitment to multiculturalism by promoting its historical, social, and musical heritage.

Savannah College of Art and Design, which serves about 2,500 students, grants bachelors degrees in architecture and fine arts, as well as the Master of Fine Arts degree. The college has an unusual campus, with classrooms and dormitories housed in approximately 30 restored buildings located throughout Savannah's Historic District. Additionally, the college, its students and faculty add a great sense of vitality and economic base to downtown.

Savannah Technical Institute, governed by the Savannah Chatham County Board of Public Education and the Georgia Department of Technical and Adult Education, offers classes on five campuses, serving over 8,400 community members annually.

Privately owned South College has 550 students enrolled who can earn two-year degrees as paralegals, medical assistants, computer operators, or executive secretaries. Graduates go directly into the work force, or use their courses towards a four-year degree at another college or university.

Improving education is also a high priority of the business community, since a strong school system is critical when recruiting workers or attracting new business to the area.

A Vision of Prosperity

When Lady Astor visited in 1946, she called Savannah "a lovely lady with a dirty face." The comment was true at the time, but Savannahians have worked wonders since then sprucing up the beautiful city they love.

"Savannah is the Mother city of Georgia, but in 1960, it was a city of old, dilapidated, blighted buildings," says city manager Arthur A. "Don" Mendonsa. "There wasn't even a good thoroughfare. Tourism wasn't an industry. We were little more than a mill town. Today, the slums have been cleared, the Historic District has been restored, the streets are paved, and tourism is booming. When you consider all of that, Savannah has made gigantic leaps."

And work continues. Historic Savannah is in the midst of a five-year program that will return Bull Street—the main artery of the Historic District, featuring some of the loveliest squares and a happy mix of homes and businesses—to the glory of its finest days. A volunteer effort, much like the one that restored the Forsyth Park fountain, is ready to take on the restoration of the

16-mile Savannah-Ogeechee Canal, built during the 1820s, and reopen it as a recreational area for canoeing, boating, hiking, walking, and picnicking.

Dreamed about, but not yet pinned down, are plans for the redevelopment of the former downtown shopping hub, Broughton Street, and construction of a convention center, both necessary for continued downtown growth. Then, too, there are the human issues that must be addressed.

Much of what needs to be done—economically, environmentally, and socially—to ensure the best Savannah that can be is contained in a report called Vision 20/20 orchestrated by Arnold Tenenbaum, a businessman and civic leader.

"Vision 20/20 was a way of bringing the community together in a more collaborative approach than had been done before," Tenenbaum explains. "We identified specific areas that need improvement and developed a blueprint for action. We collaborated with the city, the county, the schools, the Savannah Economic Development Authority, and the Chamber. We narrowed the focus and identified a work plan year by year. Vision 20/20 is a citizens' lobbying voice. It's the direction we know we need to go to solve our problems. The next step is to begin implementation, and we have already selected the person to lead that phase."

Savannah has everything going for it, Tenenbaum says: "It's beautiful. The location on the water gives us the opportunity to lead such a fantastic lifestyle. And we have business leaders who care about what is best for the community. Essentially, the business community wants to see a prosperity come to this area and wants to see *all* of the citizens share in that prosperity."

W.W. Law, a lifelong advocate of African-American interests, is cautiously optimistic about the future of blacks in Savannah. He cites recent positives: The rehabilitation of the oldest black neighborhood in the city, Beach Institute Historic Neighborhood, is bringing young blacks back into the inner city. Jazz enthusiast Ben Tucker is reviving "an interest in good entertainment."

Savannah State College continues in its role to develop new African-American leadership. Still, the road for some of the city's poorest citizens is not easy, says Law:

"There is an old song: 'All the way to heaven, ups and downs, ups and downs. Rocks on every hand.' The history of blacks has been ups and downs. It is not an easy path. But we have been in Savannah since day one, and we will be here yet. This can be a great life if we come together. I see from time to time a ray of light, and we must keep on keeping on."

Dennis Smith, vice president of sales for Carson Products, sees younger blacks becoming more and more comfortable with the past: "There are some young people who have been uneasy about the antebellum past, but we were there and we were a part of it. We are not invisible, and I think we need to highlight the good things we've done. Pride in the past will help us make contributions in the future."

Oddly enough, it may be Savannah's role as hostess city for the yachting events during the 1996 Olympic Games that may well be the impetus for improvements that will benefit all Savannahians.

"What this means is exposure and recognition on a scale that we've never ever had," says Archie Davis, chairman of SOSCO, the Savannah Olympic Support Council, whose job it is to function as a catalyst, coordinator, and implementor of programs that will support the Olympic games. SOSCO has key areas it believes are important, among them: beautification efforts, soliciting volunteers, coordinating pre-festivals and events, and helping minority and small businesses land some of the lucrative contracts that will be coming Savannah's way.

It is estimated that 3 billion people will tune in to watch the sailing competitions in Savannah. More than 15,000 journalists will cover the Olympics, with 200 specifically assigned to spend 17 days in Savannah.

"I can't begin to quantify the economic impact this exposure can have on Savannah, and what that recognition will bring," says Davis. "There are 191 countries involved in the Olympics, and 70 of them have sailing events. The Olympics will make us a destination for sailing rather than a transit point."

The Chamber's John Hicks agrees: "We've had a huge bonanza dropped in our laps. People with investments to make will have their attention focused on us for the first time ever, and we will have the chance to fix ourselves in their memories."

Carolyn Donovan, a Savannahian who was part of the three-year effort to bring the Olympics to Savannah, believes visitors will not be disappointed in what they find here: "People who are expecting to see the Old South can see that in Savannah, and they will be totally charmed by it. The Europeans especially can relate to it. It's where they feel at home.

"I learned through this effort that winning the Olympic bid wasn't about hotel rooms or airports. It was about doing what we do well in this part of the country—getting to know people, making them feel welcome and comfortable, making them feel at home."

Savannahians are historically tied to this enchanting place they call home. They know they live in one of the most beautiful places on earth, and, as always, they are anxious to share it with company.

Oddly enough, it may be Savannah's role as hostess city for the yachting events during the 1996 Olympic Games that may well be the impetus for improvements that will benefit all Savannahians.

In 1991, the 37-year-old Talmadge Memorial Bridge (right) was replaced by a new bridge (far right) that increased clearance on the Savannah River from 137 feet to 185 feet, opening the harbor to 98 percent of the world's shipping fleet.

Following pages:
This is not the "Moon River" of
Savannahian and Academy
Award-winning songwriter
Johnny Mercer, but the harbor
scene is certainly lyrical in its
own way. A full moon over the
Savannah River lights the way
for ships from all over the world.
Photo: Joseph Byrd

Total construction costs of Savannah's new bridge topped $70 million. The old bridge, seen in the shadows, was dismantled, and portions of the steel frame were taken to sea, where it is hoped they will serve as reefs thriving with game fish.

The Georgia Ports Authority terminals attract more than 1,600 ships yearly from 250 ports representing 160 countries. Savannah River traffic also includes hundreds more ships that arrive at privately owned terminals. Savannah is the second-ranking port, behind Jacksonville, Florida, in total tonnage on the South Atlantic.

There is a golden glow to Savannah, such as the early morning sun against a stuccoed wall, or River Street lanterns outside The Chart House restaurant, located in one of the oldest cotton warehouses along the riverfront.

River Street glistens at dawn, a time when ships, bars, and restaurants are quiet before the onslaught of midday. The rails that run along the ballast stone-lined street carry the River Street Rambler, a working freight train that makes a daily run from the port to businesses along the track.

Wares for the start of another business day are unloaded along the bricked sidewalk in front of the Hyatt Regency on River Street, a popular setting for a number of city-sponsored events.

The Palmer & Cay/Carswell
building, a modern rendering in
stucco, and the First Union
Bank, a handsome turn-of-the-
century structure, show that new
and old architecture can coexist
beautifully on Johnson Square,
which has been the business
hub of downtown since
Savannah's beginning.

Tinted windows of the modern Trust Company Bank in Johnson Square reflect details of the First Union Bank building, which, when lit up at night, is Savannah's Parthenon.

A griffin fountain stands guard outside the Savannah Cotton Exchange, completed in 1887 during the time when 2 million bales of cotton moved through the port yearly and the Exchange was teeming with clerks, factors, and exporters. The Cotton Exchange (opposite) is now the home of Solomon's Lodge, which was organized as a masonic order in 1734 and is today one of the oldest in the United States.

▼ JOSEPH BYRD

During the winter of 1865, General William Tecumseh Sherman set up headquarters in the Gothic Revival mansion of Charles Green. Designed by Charles Norris, it was built in the 1850s for $93,000. Known as the Green-Meldrim House, the building has served since 1943 as the parish house for St. John's Episcopal Church (opposite), built in 1852-53 in a complementary Gothic Revival style.

Churchgoing is an important part of the fabric of Savannah life. The city's many historic churches include the Cathedral of St. John the Baptist (top right), an immense French Gothic style cathedral that could be seen by the young Flannery O'Connor, who grew up across the street.

The First African Baptist Church (top left) was begun in 1773 and is one of the oldest black congregations in the United States. The present building, with stained glass added in 1885, was erected by church members in 1859.

Christ Church (bottom left) was the first church established in the colony in 1733, at Johnson Square, the first square. The present church building was erected in 1837 and rebuilt in 1897 after it was gutted by fire. John Wesley is reported to have begun the first Sunday schools in America at Christ Church and at the church at New Ebenezer, a settlement of Salzburgers near Savannah.

Independent Presbyterian Church (bottom right), a replica of its 1819 predecessor, was erected in 1890 after the original structure burned the previous year. Woodrow Wilson married Ellen Axson, granddaughter of the pastor, in the manse of the church in 1885.

JOHN CARRINGTON, *SAVANNAH NEWS-PRESS*

CHARLES RIBBENS

CHARLES RIBBENS

JOSEPH BYRD

The Temple Mickve Israel congregation was organized in 1733 and received its charter in 1790, making it the third oldest Jewish congregation in America and the oldest in the South. The stuccoed temple, in Gothic Revival style, was completed in 1878.

In among Savannah's expansive architectural vistas, there are many details worthy of note, such as this stained glass window on Abercorn Street and a nearby doorknob.

▼ STEVE BISSON, *SAVANNAH NEWS-PRESS*

Following pages:
A sultry summer day often leads to violent lightning, which appears to strike the spires of the Cathedral of St. John the Baptist (left).
Photo: Joseph Trotz, Savannah News-Press

The Tybee Lighthouse (right) shines through the mist, warning ships that they are near the Georgia coastline. The top part of the lighthouse was destroyed during the Civil War, so today, the lower 60 feet date back to 1773, and the upper 94 feet date to 1867. The lighthouse is maintained by the Tybee Island Historical Society and is an active aid to navigation.
Photo: Joseph Shields

The Savannah College of Art and
Design, with an enrollment of
2,000-plus students, conducts
classes in the Georgia Volunteer
Guard Armory, a Romanesque
Revival building erected in 1892.
The college has exhibited style,
good taste, and community
commitment in adapting more
than 30 downtown buildings
for use as classrooms and
dormitories.

Savannah's numerous spring showers bring out May flowers and an abundance of colorful umbrellas.

Savannah in the spring means dogwoods with dainty blossoms and azaleas bursting with wild color, contrasting with orderly Gaston Street row houses. Row houses, so designed because Oglethorpe's city plan allowed for lots that were narrow and deep, sometimes run for whole city blocks. The main living quarters were typically raised a story off the ground to avoid the grime from dusty streets.

▼ *JOHN CARRINGTON, SAVANNAH NEWS-PRESS*

64

This Italianate Hall Street residence, built in 1884, has been featured on one of several annual home tours held in Savannah when the city is loveliest, during the holidays and the spring. The impressive wrought iron is of Chippendale design.

The Richardson-Owens-Thomas House at 124 Abercorn Street is run by the Telfair Academy of Arts and Sciences as a house museum. It was designed by English architect William Jay and is considered one of the best preserved and finest examples of his work in the nation. The house was completed in 1819, and has been painstakingly decorated in period furnishings.

JOSEPH BYRD

Hodgson Hall (left), which looks out over Forsyth Park from Whitaker Street, is the home of the Georgia Historical Society, founded in 1839. The hall, built for the society in 1875, houses manuscripts, rare books, public records, maps, photographs, prints, portraits, artifacts, newspapers, periodicals, and genealogical resources that document Georgia's history from the earliest days.

Flamboyant Juliette Gordon Low, founder of the Girl Scout movement, was born in the Wayne-Gordon House (right) at 142 Bull Street on Halloween, 1860. This Regency style house, built in 1818 and altered considerably through the years, is now the national program center for the Girl Scouts. It is open for tours and has been elegantly restored to the late 1800s period, featuring many family furnishings.

JOSEPH BYRD

CHARLES RIBBENS

Although James Edward Oglethorpe was not made a general until 1765, after his return to England, he is immortalized in Savannah's Chippewa Square in the full dress of a British general, a sword in his hand, a palm frond at his feet. Four lions guard the bronze image of the man who established Georgia as America's 13th colony.

From 1753 until 1850, Colonial Cemetery was the only burial spot in Savannah. Button Gwinnett, one of three Georgians to sign the Declaration of Independence, is thought to be buried there, killed in a duel in 1777. Wrought iron and old brick encircle the park, and a bronze eagle with wings outspread adds drama to the stone gateway. The cemetery was restored in 1967 by the Trustees' Garden Club and is a favorite spot for moody walks down tabby lanes by tourists and locals alike.

This magnificent oak alley stretches for more than a mile, ending at the tabby remains of Wormsloe, a colonial estate constructed by Noble Jones, one of Savannah's original settlers. The Isle of Hope plantation is a state historic site and is open to the public.

▼ GREGORY WILLIAMS

Weather-beaten and leafless, a live oak skeleton stands on Wassaw, one of the area's barrier islands and a critical nesting ground for sea turtles.

Cattle egrets feed around the cows that roam the grounds of Bethesda, founded on the Isle of Hope in 1740 by the Rev. George Whitefield as the first orphanage in America. Today, the Bethesda cottages and pastoral setting serve as a temporary home to boys whose families are in crisis.

▼ R.T. FULLER

KAREN ROEDER

Alligators in the wild do not live in groups, but those in captivity at Oatland Island Education Center are willing to share their marshy quarters. All of the natural animal habitats for the center, owned and operated by the Chatham-Savannah public school system, were constructed by students.

CHARLES RIBBENS

Volunteers of the Caretta Research Project are credited with saving from extinction the threatened loggerhead sea turtle. Females of the ancient species return every two years in June or July to the same spot to nest, depositing a clutch of about 124 golf ball-size eggs before returning to the sea. Volunteers guard the nests until the baby loggerheads hatch and make their treacherous path to the ocean. The turtle pictured here is covered with barnacles that live exclusively on loggerheads.

Savannah is in the midst of active nesting grounds for many marsh birds, including the Moore hen.

This immature heron will grow into an elegant wading bird that will savor the aquatic food the Lowcountry rivers and creeks provide. Throughout the coastal area, wading birds—egrets, herons, ibis, and endangered wood storks—are easily spotted. Shore birds—pelicans, terns, and gulls—play and feed along the beach.

Following pages:
Fifteen minutes from downtown is the 26,000-acre Savannah National Wildlife Refuge, where dry dog fennel rustling in the wind and songbirds on the way up and down the coast are the sounds that have dominated the land for generations.
Photo: Peter J. Campbell

A child of the Lowcountry often learns to fish before he learns to ride a bicycle, and to clean a blue crab before he enters kindergarten. Such are the privileges of coastal life.

Few afternoons are more satisfying than those spent savoring the sand, sun, and surf on Tybee Island.

Shrimpers at Thunderbolt, Georgia, have earned their livelihoods for generations from the bounty of the sea. More than a million pounds of shrimp are caught annually in Chatham County, representing an income to shrimpers of more than $4 million.

A shrimp boat heads out through Lazaretta Creek. The Cockspur Island lighthouse in the distance was built in 1848-1849 and was operational until 1909.

Brown and white shrimp come in from the ocean to spawn in the marshes around Savannah. Shrimpers, with their traditionally white boats, are ready for them when they do.

Ship-watching from River Street is best experienced in silence. A close look reveals beauty in even the smallest details, like this worn ship's anchor.

Following pages:
A mild climate year-round makes Coastal Georgia ideal for sailing (left), a sport that will be featured when Savannah hosts the sailing competitions of the Olympic Games in the summer of 1996.
Photo: Joseph Byrd

Navigational charts (right) are necessary for fishermen and pleasure boaters who want to travel the Intracoastal Water-way and the hundreds of spidery creeks and rivers that spread beyond.
Photo: Peter J. Campbell

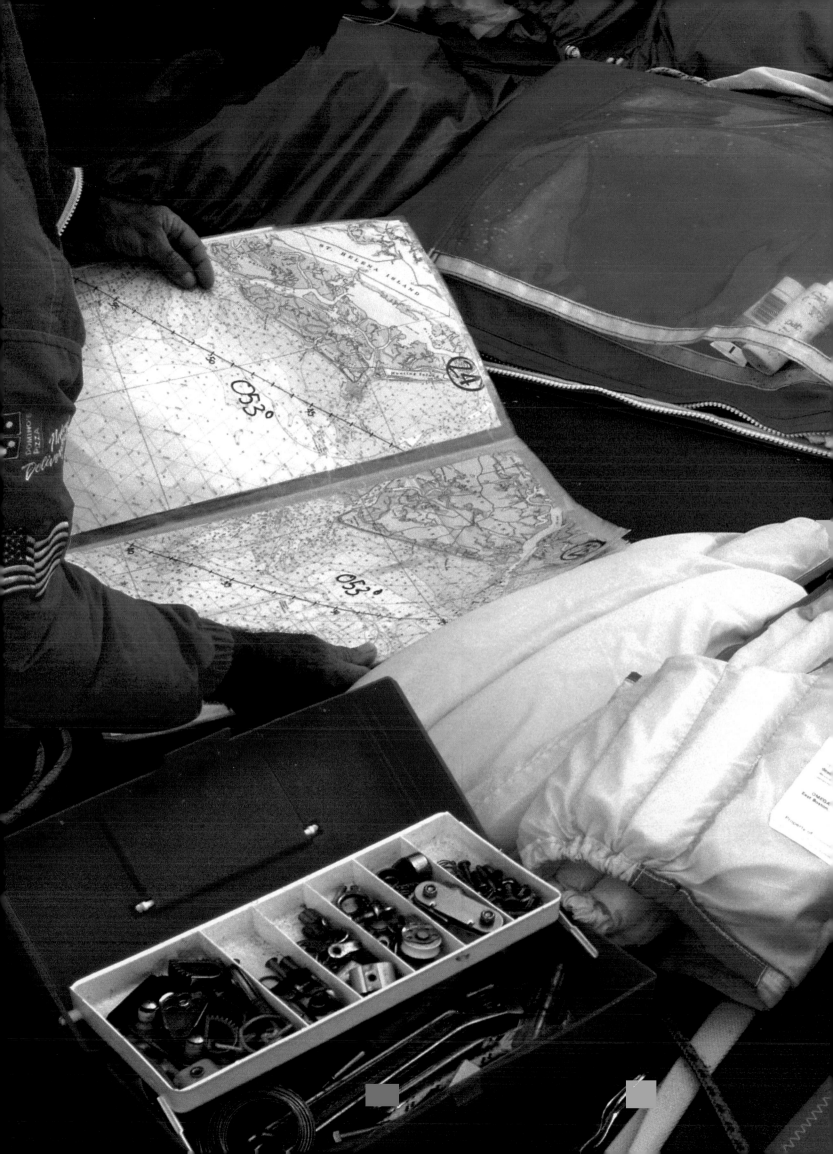

At present, there are 20 golf courses within a 50-mile radius of Savannah.

An aerial view of Phase Two of the Landings community on Skidaway Island illustrates the stunning payoff when abundant green space is planned for.

The Gulf Fritillary, a migratory butterfly that nests in Savannah, feeds on Lantana, a common plant in the Savannah summer landscape.

▼ R.T. FULLER

Savannah's azaleas come in many varieties, such as this copper-colored Flame.

Spiderwort, or dayflower, is a naturalized wildflower that blooms throughout Coastal Georgia in the spring.

The magnolia, with its luscious, fragrant blossoms, is one of the dominant trees in the maritime forest, where it has reigned with the oak for thousands of years.

Feeding geese from a safe distance makes for a pleasant afternoon at Lake Mayer, one of several Savannah-area community parks.

▼ *PAULA GOMEZ, SAVANNAH NEWS-PRESS*

Pigeons and squirrels in Forsyth Park in downtown Savannah demand to be catered to, and park regulars are always willing to oblige.

Each spring, Savannah College of Art and Design students turn concrete into canvas during the sidewalk art competition.

Bubbles, provided here by Savannah College of Art and Design students, add a sense of merriment to street festivals.

A face-painter remains steady under the gaze of an intent audience during a Forsyth Park youth festival.

It's spring, and the cameras come out in great numbers to record the season's beauty.

▼ JOHN CARRINGTON, *SAVANNAH NEWS-PRESS*

This youngster is in the pink, thanks to a visit from a friendly, bug-eyed monster who appeared during a downtown festival.

Savannah goes green for St. Patrick's Day, with as many as 300,000 revelers on hand to share the madness. The annual parade is said to be one of the largest in the country.

The city has not forgotten the teachings of Dr. Martin Luther King Jr. A march is held in his honor each year in downtown Savannah.

The founding of Georgia's first city in 1733 is remembered every February 12, when thousands of school children and adults dress in colonial costumes for a commemorative parade through the downtown squares.

JOHN CARRINGTON, *SAVANNAH NEWS-PRESS*

Historic battles are occasionally reenacted in Savannah at such sites as Fort Jackson, where cannons are fired and other notable weapons, tools, and machinery are displayed and demonstrated.

President George Bush is one of
several United States presidents
who have saluted Savannah.

JOHN CARRINGTON, *SAVANNAH NEWS-PRESS*

Maj. Gen. Barry R. McCaffrey led 26,000 soldiers of the 24th Infantry Division (Mechanized) to a decisive victory in the 100-hour ground war of Operation Desert Storm. Eight division soldiers died in the Persian Gulf war. Families were separated from loved ones for months during the conflict, and the communities of Savannah and Hinesville rallied to their support.

Benedictine Academy cadets carry on the tradition of military readiness that is one of the cornerstones of Savannah's history.

The Savannah Cardinals, the city's Class A minor league baseball team, attract a loyal following to their games at Grayson Stadium.

JOSEPH TROTZ, SAVANNAH NEWS-PRESS

"I can't begin to quantify the economic impact this exposure can have on Savannah," says Archie Davis, chairman of the Savannah Olympic Support Council, a group whose job it is to support activities leading up to the 1996 Summer Olympic Games. Davis, relaxed but ready, is pictured in the waters near Priest's Landing, where the Olympic yachting competitions will be staged. Seventy countries are expected to participate in the sailing of eight classes of boats.

The new Savannah bridge provides athletes with a breath-taking runner's high.

The Savannah State College Playhouse sets the stage for aspiring actors.

Dancers with Ballet South perform *The Nutcracker* each holiday season to the delight of audiences young and old.

Following pages: Fireworks over the Savannah River (left) cap off Fourth of July celebrations throughout the city. *Photo: R.T. Fuller*

(Right) Boaters anchored in the Savannah River have ringside seats to watch rockets burst above the new bridge. *Photo: John Carrington, Savannah News-Press*

A clown beckons riders at the 16th Street amusement park on Tybee Island.

A member of the 8th Air Force Historical Society takes the bombardier position aboard a B-17.

During the dog days of summer, people—and their best friends—long for relief from the intense heat and humidity, but they bear the burden with good humor.

▼ JOHN CARRINGTON, *SAVANNAH NEWS-PRESS*

Mrs. L.H. Wilkes (center) is famous nationwide for the country cooking—collards, corn bread, and Hoppin' John— served family-style at her board- ing house on Jones Street.

Crabbing with hand lines and chicken necks can yield a basket of blue crabs that are unmatched in taste appeal.

In May, the air around Savannah hangs heavy with the aroma of sweet Vidalia onions. The coveted onions are brought in by the truckload and savored by gourmets throughout the area.

A carpenter's sign is an example
of modern mastery with iron.

The concrete towers on the city's new bridge rise to 417 feet and are reinforced with almost 4 million pounds of steel. Bridge construction also called for 49,456 linear feet of stay cables.

GREGORY WILLIAMS

A state-of-the-art computer runs the No. 8 paper machine at Union Camp. The No. 8 annually produces 460,000 tons of linerboard, which is used to make corrugated boxes.

▼ JOSEPH BYRD

Local industries in Savannah have invested well over a billion dollars in capital improvements and equipment in recent years.

Forty percent of Savannah's economy is based in manufacturing—from foodstuffs like bread, oil, and sugar to paint dye, cardboard boxes, and corporate jets.

Workers take a break under
sunny skies that are fairly typical
in Savannah.

JOSEPH BYRD

Fortunate travelers of the Intra-coastal Waterway can dock at one of 16 marinas in the area.

Following pages:
It took 18 years, $1 million, and 25 million bricks to build Fort Pulaski, completed in 1847. Many considered the fort invincible, but during the Civil War, after 30 hours of intense bombardment by Union troops, Confederate forces surrendered. Today, the meticulously maintained fort on Cockspur Island is administered by the National Park Service and is open year-round for touring.
Photo: Charles Ribbens

The Central of Georgia Railway roundhouse and shops complex on Harris Street is a National Landmark site dedicated to railroad heritage. The city has earmarked $500,000 for capital improvements that include restoring the smokestack with specially-made Savannah grey brick— large porous brick made in the city until 1910—to duplicate the originals. The complex opens for touring in fall, 1992.

The five-and-a-half-acre round-house park includes America's oldest-known stationary steam engine, which was used to power the most complete railroad repair shops in the nation. Nearby the Savannah History Museum and Savannah Visitors' Center are housed in the Central of Georgia Railway terminal, completed in 1861.

Southern pines were almost as important to Savannah's early prosperity as cotton. Cotton was king, but naval stores—the products of pines—were next in importance. Today, pines are harvested and conscientiously replaced by Union Camp, the world's largest kraft paper mill.

JOSEPH BYRD

The Vidalia onion crop contributes $35 to $40 million a year to Georgia's economy.

Ships calling on Savannah's port
are escorted into the channel
by tugboats.

Tugboat captains have to keep a
constant eye on currents and
river traffic.

Following pages:
A ship's golden hull is nudged by
a tug, while a giant crane lifts
cargo in the misty distance.
Savannah was, and still is, a great
port city.
Photo: Joseph Byrd

PROFILES IN

BY POLLY POWERS STRAMM
A look at the corporations, businesses, professional groups, and community service organizations that have made this book possible.

Early in September 1779, a French naval armada, led by Charles-Henri, Comte D'Estaing, arrived to aid Americans in destroying Britain's military power. On October 9, 1779, 3,000 American and French forces were involved in a bloody assault called the Siege of Savannah. The Allies, sustaining heavy casualties, were repulsed after 55 minutes of fighting.

GEORGIA HISTORICAL SOCIETY

EXCELLENCE

1 8 0 0

1803
Candler General Hospital

1806
Savannah Area Chamber of Commerce

1845
Solomons Company

1868
Palmer & Cay/Carswell, Inc.

1869
First Union National Bank of Georgia

The Forsyth Park fountain was the center of activity in this photograph taken in 1868. The cast-iron fountain was erected in 1858 in a design similar to the grand Paris fountain in the Place de la Concorde. It was renovated in 1988 and continues to be one of Savannah's most cherished landmarks.

1 8 8 5

1875
Saint Joseph's Hospital

1879
*Hunter, Maclean, Exley &
Dunn, P.C.*

1882
*Savannah Electric & Power
Company*

1885
*Hilb, Rogal & Hamilton Company
of Savannah*

▶ GEORGIA HISTORICAL SOCIETY

This eastward view shows Savannah's port at its heyday, around 1890. Cotton merchants located offices and counting houses along Factors' Row or Factors' Walk. Although the buildings appear to be only two stories high from this angle, they were actually five stories high on the river side. In the center of the row is the Savannah Cotton Exchange, constructed in 1886 as a world center for the cotton trade.

Candler General Hospital

S avannah's most historic hospital is also one of the region's most progressive health care providers.

Candler General Hospital traces its family tree to the Savannah Poor House and Hospital, created in 1808 just 75 years after English General James Edward Oglethorpe founded the Savannah colony. Renamed Warren A. Candler Hospital in 1930 in honor of a Georgia Methodist bishop, the facility became Candler General Hospital in 1967 and in 1980 moved from downtown Savannah to new facilities near the geographical heart of the city. From its historic roots, Candler has grown into a 335-bed center for advanced health care and the centerpiece of an expanding network of services for southeast Georgia, Candler Health Services, Inc.

More than 77,000 new lives have entered the world as "Telfair babies" during the unit's century-long history.

Candler today strives to fulfill its role as a premier regional health care provider by linking medical breakthroughs with an advanced medical team. More than brick and mortar housing high technology, Candler represents the combined resources of a multi-specialty medical and dental staff, a nursing staff encouraged to seek national certification, and highly skilled ancillary staff members in other diagnostic and treatment areas—all backed by a battery of support services. Continuing education helps Candler's professionals hone their expertise and stay abreast of the latest developments in modern medicine.

Right: Candler General Hospital is a 335-bed center providing a range of advanced medical services to citizens throughout southeast Georgia.

STAYING ON THE LEADING EDGE

To help meet the diverse health care needs of the more than 500,000 citizens in its service area, Candler provides an expanding range of services, including obstetrics and gynecology, oncology, orthopedics, rehabilitation, respiratory care, emergency medicine, urology, and ear, nose, and throat medicine. Diagnostic support services such as magnetic resonance imaging, computed tomography, ultrasound, nuclear medicine, cardiac catheterization, electrocardiology, and pathology services complement the treatment side of patient care.

More than 12,000 surgical procedures are performed at Candler every year. Medical advancements like surgical lasers and laparoscopy often mean surgery with less pain, fewer complications, lower cost, and shorter hospital stays for patients at Candler. In fact, Candler set the pace for the use of laser-supported surgery with the city's first Neodymium-Yttrium-Aluminum-Garnet (Nd:YAG) laser, the first in an expanding line of advanced surgical

laser systems used at the hospital for everything from eye to orthopedic surgery.

In 1990, another first came to Savannah when surgeons at Candler performed a laser laparoscopic cholecystectomy to remove a diseased gall bladder. At the time, Candler was one of only 20 hospitals in the United States to offer the procedure in which the surgeon inserts a laser, a fiber-optic camera, and other surgical tools through a tiny incision while performing surgery. Laparoscopy provides surgeons a welcome option to more traditional, more invasive surgical techniques for treating a variety of medical conditions.

Innovation in both care and technology also shapes Candler's services for pregnant women and newborns, a hallmark of the hospital since the Telfair Hospital for Females opened more than a century ago. Savannah patron and philanthropist Mary Telfair had long wished for a medical facility to serve the women of the community. Following her death in 1875, her wish was finally fulfilled through her estate. In 1886, the Telfair opened on Park Avenue just south of Forsyth Park. It was incorporated into Candler Hospital in 1960 after operating from its original buildings for nearly 75 years. When Candler moved to new facilities in 1980, the Telfair was relocated to the third floor of the hospital.

More than 77,000 new lives have entered the world as "Telfair babies" during the unit's century-long history. Today, Candler approaches childbirth not as an illness, but as a normal, healthy experience.

That caring philosophy is reflected in the Telfair Family Maternity Center's labor-delivery-recovery suites or LDRs. Remodeled and expanded in 1992, the unit's LDRs look more like a combination bedroom and

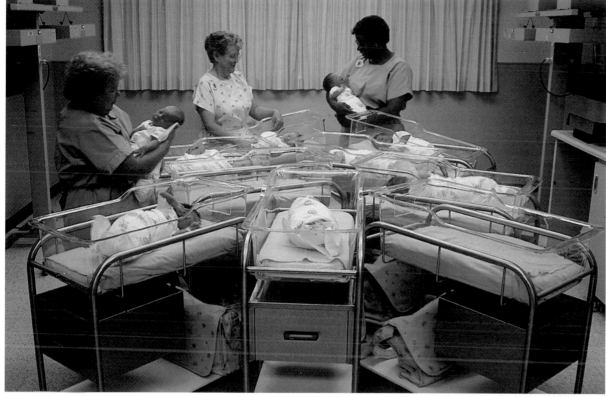

Today, new mothers choose from a variety of birthing options available in the new labor-delivery-recovery suites of Candler's Telfair Family Maternity Center.

nursery than a hospital room. Each suite is spacious and cheerful with touches like a rocking chair, private bath, entertainment center, vanity and dressing area, and other amenities for parents and babies. Although concealed by artwork, fabrics, and carefully chosen colors, the finest technology is available in every LDR to monitor and help care for both new mothers and Candler's tiniest patients. When surgery is required for obstetrical or gynecological conditions, state-of-the-art surgery suites are only a few feet away within the Telfair.

Complementing the third-floor Telfair Family Maternity Center is the Telfair Pavilion, located in the Candler Professional Building adjacent to the hospital. This outpatient center provides a range of diagnostic and educational services for women, including nationally accredited mammography, ultrasound examination, osteoporosis screening and classes, seminars, and support groups of interest to women throughout the Coastal Empire.

Candler's nationally accredited rehabilitation program was established in 1970 as a stroke unit after local physicians detected an excessive rate of high blood pressure in the Savannah area. In 1971, Candler was designated the Areawide Stroke Facility by the Georgia Regional Medical Program and has helped the region realize a significant reduction in deaths from stroke.

The Rehabilitation Unit was eventually opened in 1984 as a separate unit within the hospital and is today accredited by the Commission on Accreditation of Rehabilitation Facilities. The unit provides rehabilitation services for persons who have suffered strokes or heart attacks, who experience chronic pain, or who have undergone surgery and require rehabilitation during recovery. Rehabilitation teams of physicians, nurses, dietitians, social workers, chaplains, and an appropriate combination of occupational, physical, and recreational therapists typify the multidisciplinary approach Candler takes to many types of patient care.

A NETWORK FOR THE '90S AND BEYOND

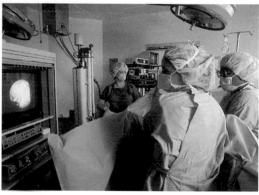

Candler offers a variety of diagnostic and treatment resources to physicians on the medical and dental staff.

Candler extends and expands its services to the community and region through its parent company, Candler Health Services (CHS). CHS acts as the umbrella organization for affiliates, partnerships, and programs that deliver such diverse services as managed care, home health care, clinical laboratory services, around-the-clock personal emergency response systems, radiation therapy for cancer patients, child care, and more.

Recognizing the importance of southeast Georgia's rural hospitals to the region's total health care delivery system, CHS has also established links with a growing number of smaller hospitals. While the individual facilities retain their independence, the services they provide to their communities and neighboring counties are strengthened through their access to Candler's resources.

As it has for almost two centuries, the Candler family will continue to be an active partner in the good health of Savannah, Chatham County, and southeast Georgia as the region stands on the threshold of a new century.

Solomons Company

With a rich tradition of service to customers and the community, Solomons Company is a regional leader in the wholesale drug industry. Founded almost 150 years ago by Abraham Alexander Solomons, the company does business with more than 500 drugstores and hospitals.

Remaining strong in the wholesale drug business today is challenging, even for the most stable companies. Despite dramatic increases in total sales, the industry has consolidated from 147 firms to 83 in just the past 15 years.

Company president Philip Solomons Jr., great-great-grandson of the founder, explains, "Solomons Company has survived and thrived by combining old-fashioned personal service with the best new technologies, providing products and services that enable our customers to succeed. We treat our customers, our employees, and our suppliers with fairness and respect."

"I guess the reason we have resisted selling the company," he adds, "is the family's philosophy of stewardship: take care of the business every day, and it will be there to take care of you."

A RICH HISTORY IN SAVANNAH

The Solomons family and their business have met challenges and overcome obstacles for generations. Founder A.A. Solomons, a native of Georgetown, South Carolina, was only 14 years old when his father died in 1830. As the oldest of eight children, he bore much of the financial responsibility for his widowed mother and siblings. By age 19, he had been licensed by the Medical Society of South Carolina to "...carry on the business of Apothecary and Druggist." In 1845, he moved to Savannah and established an apothecary shop.

The Solomons' dedication to their business and the community was evident from the beginning—even in the face of hardship or danger. During the Civil War, all pharmaceuticals were considered contraband. Quinine was so scarce that blockade runners risked their lives to obtain this medication used for treating malaria. Despite the danger, the Savannah Benevolent Association and the Solomons family were able to secure, compound, and dispense quinine to the troops. Written correspondence from General Robert E. Lee and Alexander H. Stephens remains a cherished part of the company's heritage.

The war, however, took a financial toll on the company as A.A. Solomons struggled to keep it in operation. After Lee's surrender, Solomons traveled north to meet with the firm's creditors, many of whom were the country's largest drug manufacturers. These firms, trusting that the family's steadfastness and integrity would see the company through, allowed Solomons to hold on to his small business.

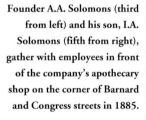

Founder A.A. Solomons (third from left) and his son, I.A. Solomons (fifth from right), gather with employees in front of the company's apothecary shop on the corner of Barnard and Congress streets in 1885.

In 1876, the company faced yet another challenge as the yellow fever epidemic swept through Savannah. In a little over a month's time, 5,542 cases were reported. By the epidemic's end, more than half of Savannah's 30,000 residents had either died or fled the city. Once again, Solomons Company and the Benevolent Association joined forces to see the community through the crisis.

Over time, Solomons developed the wholesale end of the business. In 1939, in order to focus all its efforts on wholesaling, the family sold its famous apothecary shop at the corner of Bull and Charlton streets. The company continued to grow, acquiring Savannah drug wholesalers Reeves-McTeer in 1963 and Columbia Drug in 1971.

Today, in addition to Philip Solomons Jr., four other descendants of the founder help operate the company: Philip Solomons Sr., who guided the company through its two acquisitions and emergence as a regional leader, is chairman of the board; his wife, Shirley, is secretary/ treasurer; and their sons, Richard and Ralph, oversee the purchasing and returns departments, respectively.

Truly a "family business," among the current 170 employees are seven husband-and-wife teams, only one of which is in the Solomons family. There are also several employees who represent the second generation of their families to work for the company.

A SERVICE-ORIENTED COMPANY

Solomons Company carries a full line of pharmaceuticals and a broad range of non-pharmaceutical products—over 30,000 different items—and delivers them overnight to approximately 100 hospitals and 400 drugstores in Georgia, South Carolina, and Florida.

"For the small difference in price between ordering from us and ordering directly from the manufacturer," says Solomons, "customers can get everything from one source, electronically, and receive their orders within 24 hours, with pricing labels customized to each customer's specifications."

As today's hospitals seek to better utilize space and reduce the dollars tied up in their drug inventories, they depend heavily on Solomons' high levels of service.

A special service which Solomons provides to independently owned retail pharmacies is a co-operative advertising program. With over 160 drugstores partici-

A longtime tradition of family involvement survives at Solomons Company today. From left: Philip Jr., Ralph, Philip Sr., Shirley, and Richard.

pating, the company is able to make volume purchases on selected items at especially low prices. Solomons passes these prices on to the drugstores, who in turn pass them along to their customers. Each month, Solomons creates special advertising which, when combined with the low prices, allows independent pharmacies to compete with regional and national chain stores.

With its spacious 84,000-square-foot facility, 30-truck delivery fleet, advanced information-processing systems, and talented and dedicated employees, the company is well-positioned to provide these and other support services.

IN THE COMMUNITY TODAY

Although in recent years the company has not been called on to help battle epidemics or smuggle medication, Solomons remains actively involved in Savannah community life. "Employee participation in civic and charitable organizations and activities is extremely high," says Solomons. "I guess our concept of stewardship extends to the community and beyond the immediate family to our extended employee family."

The company has weathered decades of challenge and enjoyed almost 150 years of success thanks to its characteristic innovation and dedication to service. With the extra services that Solomons provides to its customers and the courtesy and efficiency with which it delivers them, Solomons Company eagerly looks forward to the future, even as it reflects proudly on its past.

"Solomons Company has survived and thrived by combining old-fashioned personal service with the best new technologies, providing products and services that enable our customers to succeed," says Philip Solomons Jr., president. "We treat our customers, our employees, and our suppliers with fairness and respect."

Savannah Area Chamber of Commerce

September 18, 1990 was an unforgettable day in Savannah's history: It was announced that Atlanta would host the 1996 Olympic Games and that Savannah would be the site of the yachting events. The local effort to secure the Olympic yachting competition had been coordinated by the Savannah Area Chamber of Commerce, a multi-faceted organization striving to make the community a better place in which to live, work, and visit.

Spearheading such monumental efforts is just one function of the Chamber of Commerce, a voluntary organization with a membership of approximately 1,800 Savannah area business and professional firms. An independent, nonprofit, tax-paying group, the Chamber is a business association working to enhance the economic climate of the Savannah area for business growth and quality of life through programming, services, and marketing.

"The goals of the Savannah Area Chamber of Commerce are positive ones aimed at improving the city on all fronts," says Chamber President Alan Beals. "We support existing business and industry, recruit new business to the area, support industrial recruitment, and promote and refer Chamber members to the general public. We also market the city as a convention location and a destination for tourists, and we provide countless benefits and services to members."

Those benefits and services, paid for by members' annual dues, run the gamut from receiving travel business leads generated by the Chamber's Convention and Visitors Bureau to purchasing discount mailing labels. Chamber members also receive and may advertise in the organization's membership directory and Savannah Visitors Guide. In addition, they receive a media handbook with guidelines for writing news releases, a newsletter for small business owners, a general monthly newsletter, a legislative action council bulletin, a special events brochure, a facilities guide to Savannah, and a semi-annual convention calendar. The Chamber also organizes mixers and events that give members opportunities to network and discuss topics of common interest.

The Savannah Area Chamber of Commerce is composed of seven divisions: Economic Climate, Quality Work Force, Efficient Government, Business Growth, Market Relations, Organizational Development, and the Convention and Visitors Bureau. Members address these focus areas and implement plans of action by volunteering to serve on some 40 Chamber councils and committees coordinated by a 25-member staff. Among the groups currently active are the West Chatham, Southside, and Tybee Island area councils, Chatham County Business Coalition Against Drugs, Economic Outlook, Small Business Council, Maritime Council, and Business Education Partnership Program.

Since its founding in 1806, the Chamber has evolved from a civic club into a professional association that takes the lead in developing all aspects of the city's economic life. In 1976, the Chamber created the Savannah Area Convention and Visitors Bureau to help expand the lucrative tourism market in the area. "Ultimately we try to create awareness of Savannah as a desirable destination among consumers and travel trade professionals," Beals explains. "Our city has much to offer visitors in terms of history, architecture, beauty, and romantic ambience."

The Bureau has been successful in spreading the good word about Savannah. In 1991, the city enjoyed positive editorial coverage in more than 350 publications and hosted 60,060 delegates at 197 conventions, which had a local economic impact of over $20 million. More than 5 million tourists spent over $579 million in Savannah in 1991.

Over the years Chamber programs have had long-term positive effects on the city. For example, the Chamber led the effort to establish the Coastal Georgia Center for Continuing Education in Savannah; the Silent Witness Program, which allows witnesses to report information about crimes anonymously to the Savannah Police Department; and the Savannah Compact, a joint effort between businesses and the Savannah Chatham Board of Education to improve the educational performance of Savannah's young people. The Chamber has also played an instrumental role in the building of a new river bridge linking Savannah to Hutchinson Island, the successful bid for the 1996 Olympics, and passage of a one cent local option tax for roads and bridges.

A strong, effective organization with nearly 200 years of experience, the Savannah Area Chamber of Commerce seeks to encourage and create economic growth in Savannah through its greatest resource, the membership.

Right: Gould Elementary School students celebrated Savannah as the host of the 1996 Olympic Yachting Events with an all-school assembly in September 1990.

Savannah Mayor Susan Weiner (right) with the aid of Chamber Chairman Bill Daniel (center) and President Alan Beals (left) proclaim May 4, 1992 "It's Happening in Savannah" Day.

Palmer & Cay/Carswell, Inc.

Tracing its origins to the close of the Civil War, Palmer & Cay/Carswell embraces a rich and proud past. The agency, founded in 1868 by retired Confederate General Joseph E. Johnston, is today one of the largest insurance brokers in the nation.

Joe Johnston was a close friend and former West Point classmate of Robert E. Lee. Like Lee, Johnston was a native Virginian and career soldier with the U.S. Army. Because neither Lee nor Johnston could fight against their fellow Virginians, both soldiers resigned their commissions to join the Confederacy.

General Johnston's harrowing retreat from Sherman to Atlanta is considered a military masterpiece by historians. Johnston's army was outnumbered and out-gunned three to one.

After the war, Johnston settled in Savannah where he lived on Oglethorpe Avenue and worked from insurance offices on Bay Street.

Years later, at the age of 84, Johnston traveled to New York to act as an honorary pall bearer for his wartime adversary and longtime friend, William Tecumseh Sherman. It was a brutally cold day as Johnston watched the funeral procession hat in hand. When a bystander implored Johnston to put on his hat to keep warm, the General responded, "If I were in his place and he in mine, he would not put on his hat." Just as the stranger had warned, Johnston caught a cold that day. Weeks later, that cold took the life of one of the Civil War's most respected generals and Palmer & Cay/Carswell's founder.

A HERITAGE OF FAMILY COMMITMENT

In 1888, a young Phi Beta Kappa graduate of the University of Georgia joined the insurance firm started by Johnston. John D. Carswell thus began four generations of family leadership for the agency which would soon bear his name.

Another Savannah insurance agency was founded in 1915 when Armin Palmer went into business with his son-in-law, J. Eugene Cay. The agency on Bull Street quickly developed an expertise in marine and commercial insurance.

For the next 70 years, the John D. Carswell Company and Palmer & Cay grew as competitors of mutual respect. Both the Cays and the Carswells worked assiduously to make their operations an integral part of the corporate and civic fiber of Savannah.

In 1985, Palmer & Cay purchased the Georgia and Florida operations of the Carswell Company. Headquartered in Savannah, Palmer & Cay/Carswell now has offices throughout the Southeast in Georgia, Florida, and the Carolinas. Serving Main Street shop owners and Fortune 500 manufacturers, Palmer & Cay/Carswell delivers effective risk management solutions to a spectrum of complex insurance equations from employee benefits to general liability.

Entrenched in every aspect of the agency's operations are extraordinary standards for client service and claim responsiveness. Facilitating the firm's efforts are the finest insurance companies in the industry. Palmer & Cay/Carswell, acting as agents and brokers for these carriers, hires and develops the best insurance people available.

"We believe there is no better assurance for our future success than the caliber of people working for Palmer & Cay/Carswell," says John E. Cay III, agency president. Such is the century-old heritage and commitment of one of the Southeast's premier insurance brokers.

President John E. Cay III represents four generations of agency leadership.

Left: Agency founder Joseph E. Johnston (right) with Robert E. Lee during a visit to Savannah. This was the last photograph taken of General Lee.

Saint Joseph's Hospital

S aint Joseph's Hospital, founded in 1875 by Catherine McAuley's Sisters of Mercy, has historically risen to the call of Savannah's citizens and visitors.

In the late 1800s, sailors who frequented the port city posed a unique health problem. Many were stricken with yellow fever, an epidemic which prompted the opening of the Forest City Marine Hospital. As patient needs increased and the work load at the hospital grew, the Most Rev. William Gross, then Bishop of Savannah, urged the Sisters of Mercy to take over the downtown facility in June of 1875.

By today's standards, the two-story building in late 19th century Savannah was a crude attempt at offering health care to critically ill sailors. With no running water and limited equipment, the physicians and sisters nevertheless responded to the sailors' needs by giving generously of their talents, their love, and sometimes their lives.

In 1876, the Sisters of Mercy renamed the hospital Saint Joseph's Infirmary; it wasn't until May of 1901 that the name was changed to Saint Joseph's Hospital. In subsequent years, Saint Joseph's became one of the city's most respected hospitals.

GROWING WITH SAVANNAH

The hospital's original building at Taylor and Habersham streets underwent many changes to meet the increasing needs of the community. The most notable in its early history was the construction of a 40-room annex completed in 1901. That year also marked the opening of Saint Joseph's School of Nursing. By its close in 1969, the school had graduated more than 700 nurses during its 68-year history. In 1912, with a full medical staff in place, Saint Joseph's again expanded its facilities to meet the health care needs of the community. This growth continued with additional expansions in 1930 and 1941.

Saint Joseph's history includes several important "firsts." The hospital established Savannah's first psychiatric unit, St. James Hall, in the late 1940s under the guidance of Sister Mary Bride Canty, R.S.M. Prior to the unit's opening, mentally ill patients were detained in the county jail before being transferred to the state mental facility in Milledgeville, Georgia. Also noteworthy was the opening of Saint Joseph's obstetrical clinic for families of limited income. In those days, the hospital provided the lion's share of health care to the city's indigent, often receiving only 50 cents a day per patient.

The 1960s ushered in a time of reviewing the past, assessing current demands, and planning for the city's

The hospital's original building was located at the corner of Taylor and Habersham streets in Savannah.

future health care needs. Under the leadership of Sister Mary Cornile Dulohery, R.S.M., the Saint Joseph's Advisory Board determined a new direction was needed for Saint Joseph's Hospital— south. The Sisters of Mercy demonstrated their long-standing foresight and pioneering spirit by moving to Savannah's southside, an area of widely anticipated growth. On August 15, 1970 the Sisters of Mercy dedicated a new seven-story, 200-bed hospital on Mercy Boulevard. The hospital would later expand to 300 beds with the completion of the building's top two floors.

REACHING OUT TO THE COMMUNITY

In the 1980s, preventive medicine became the key phrase for cost-conscious consumers of health care. Saint Joseph's education staff took the lead by concentrating on personal health and prevention. The result was a comprehensive community education program of classes and support groups targeting major health concerns for individuals and families. Current topics include diabetes, stress management, prenatal care, cardiac rehabilitation, and smoking cessation.

Saint Joseph's philosophy that "each individual is a cherished child of God" is evident in The BirthPlace unit, a 12-bed labor, delivery, recovery, and postpartum (LDRP) unit. The homelike environment ensures comfort and privacy for parents and babies. Mothers receive the best prenatal care available through community education classes taught by the experienced staff of obstetrical nurses and physicians.

Recognizing the high rate of heart disease in the South, Saint Joseph's HeartCare Center also has taken a leading role in cardiac research and care. Hospital cardiologists are trained in the latest diagnostic procedures such as cardiac catheterization, electrophysiology studies, and atherectomy, as well as in basic cardiopulmonary medicine. St. Joseph's cardiovascular and thoracic surgeons have many years of experience in heart surgery—experience surpassed only by their dedication and compassion for their patients.

Examples of important cardiac research at the hospital are abundant as well. Physicians are currently studying thrombolytic agents used to unclog blocked arteries, and Saint Joseph's HeartCare Center was selected as Savannah's sponsor for the National Heart Attack Risk Study, a five-year study of key risk factors for heart disease which is suffered today by a half million Americans.

As a full-service hospital, Saint Joseph's has specialties in orthopedics, oncology, neurology, urology, and emergency and general surgery.

The hospital's fourth floor is dedicated to orthopedic care, from spinal abnormalities to total joint replacements. Video-assisted laproscopic knee surgery and spine fixation devices such as TSRH Implementation, Harrington rods, Zielke screws, and spinal fusion techniques have revolutionized orthopedics at Saint Joseph's Hospital.

The sixth floor is reserved for the diagnosis and treatment of oncology patients. Outpatient and inpatient chemotherapy is available at the hospital, and outpatient radiation therapy is provided at the Savannah Oncology Center on Eisenhower Drive. Ongoing patient care includes weekly meetings of the Cancer Support Group for patients and their families to discuss needs and problems.

Treatment for critically ill patients is provided in a variety of specialized units for intensive, coronary, neuro, telemetry, and progressive care. Each unit is unique in the types of diagnosis and treatment available for specific illnesses or injuries.

HEALTH CARE EXCELLENCE FOR THE FUTURE

For more than a century, Saint Joseph's Hospital has weathered the tides of change with grace and strength. During this time, Saint Joseph's Hospital and the Sisters of Mercy have forged a special relationship with the city of Savannah—a union fostered by hard work, respect, and over a century of trust.

Today, Saint Joseph's Hospital proudly stands as a 305-bed facility housing modern technology and a dedicated team of health care professionals. The hospital's most recent expansion, a two-story outpatient addition completed in 1991, provides for expanded services in day surgery, emergency care, physical medicine, and oto-neurology.

As the health care needs of the community grow more diverse each day, so do the demands increase for hospitals to provide quality health care that is affordable. Saint Joseph's mission is to continue addressing these needs and demands. Saint Joseph's Hospital and its employees are a vital part of a community that cares about its citizens.

Today, Saint Joseph's Hospital proudly stands as a 305-bed facility housing modern technology and a dedicated team of health care professionals.

First Union National Bank of Georgia

The First Union Bank building has been a landmark on the city's horizon since its completion in 1912. *(Photo: Grant Compton)*

First Union National Bank of Georgia has adopted a strategy to position itself as a leader in sales success, total customer satisfaction, and continual development of a professional work force.

According to Rob Hoak, city president of First Union in Savannah, the key phrase at the bank these days is "total customer satisfaction." What that boils down to, he explains, is simply "bread-and-butter banking"—calling on prospective customers, serving existing customers well, and being knowledgeable about handling and pricing transactions. By adhering to these basics of successful banking, First Union strives daily to live up to its advertising slogan: "When it comes to service, *everything* matters."

OVER A CENTURY OF SERVICE IN SAVANNAH

Customer satisfaction is nothing new to First Union, which traces its local roots to Savannah Bank and Trust Co. Founded in 1869, that original entity was the oldest bank in the city and the oldest trust company in Georgia when it merged with First Railroad and Banking Co. in 1984. In 1986, First Railroad merged with First Union Corp., a holding company headquartered in Charlotte, North Carolina. At that time, Savannah Bank and Trust became part of First Union National Bank of Georgia.

First Union Corp. quickly benefited from the bank's sound reputation for financial stability and its historic physical presence in the city. In fact, Savannah Bank and Trust Co. was one of only three local financial institutions to survive the Great Depression of the 1930s. The 15-story Savannah Bank building on Johnson Square, now occupied by First Union, has been a landmark on the city's horizon since it was completed in 1912.

Right: First Union's board of directors supports the bank's commitment to "total customer satisfaction."

FOCUSED ON CUSTOMER SERVICE AND EMPLOYEE EXCELLENCE

In the first few years after the merger, First Union Corp. turned its attention toward building a single, efficient, effective statewide company by consolidating offices and converting systems. With that phase complete, the fine tuning is well under way toward becoming a leader in sales, service, and employee professionalism. To that end, First Union has set up ongoing contests among employees at its 11 Savannah branches. The sales competition rewards individual and group performance with incentive dollars.

In addition, First Union employees have developed the "Seven Keys to Total Customer Satisfaction," a list of priorities and principles to guide them in their efforts. At the top of the list is the most important key—serving the customer. Second, employees believe that superior customer service is best provided through valued and well-supported staff members. The remaining five keys assert that employees will take personal responsibility for satisfying customer needs; that they will treat customers with warmth, sincerity, honesty, and integrity; that they will strive to exceed customers' expectations—every time, all the time; that regardless of customers' demands, expectations, or behavior, the bank's goal is total customer satisfaction; and that the sole judge of satisfaction is the customer.

"The past few years of economic uncertainty have been challenging ones for the banking industry," says Hoak. "But maintaining a positive outlook is something First Union can afford to do; with our vast resources, we have become the 11th largest holding company in the United States."

Today, First Union Corp. operates more than 1,000 statewide banking offices in North Carolina, South Carolina, Georgia, and Florida, a banking office in Tennessee, and nonbanking offices in 36 states. The corporation's principal subsidiaries are its banking operations; a mortgage banking subsidiary, First Union Mortgage Corp.; a home equity lending subsidiary, First Union Home Equity Corp.; and a discount brokerage, First Union Brokerage Services, Inc. Other divisions offer consumer and commercial banking services, insurance, investment banking, and capital management products.

The sound banking strategy and tradition of excellence that Savannah Bank began in 1869 are stronger than ever today at First Union. With employee dedication to service, energetic management support, and a solid financial foundation, First Union National Bank of Georgia is prepared to further its reputation as a banking leader in Savannah and beyond.

JOSEPH BYRD

Hunter, Maclean, Exley & Dunn, P.C.

Tracing its origins to 1879 and located in historic downtown Savannah, the law firm of Hunter, Maclean, Exley & Dunn, P.C. is a growth-oriented firm, committed to the aggressive use of technology and human resources to efficiently and economically deliver legal services to its clients. The firm is also dedicated to the continuing development of new practice areas so as to better serve its existing clients and to add to its client base in southeast Georgia, adjoining South Carolina and Florida, and beyond. With roots in the past, the firm looks forward to the 21st century.

Hunter, Maclean, Exley & Dunn is the largest law firm in Georgia outside Atlanta. Its 45 attorneys practice in numerous areas of law, including general litigation, health law, toxic torts, admiralty, banking, corporate, tax, estate planning, trusts and estates, bankruptcy, environmental, employment, and real estate. While much of the firm's litigation practice is defense-oriented, especially in the areas of medical malpractice, toxic torts, and products liability, the firm also engages in plaintiff's work. The firm's diverse client roster includes banks, a railroad, members of the local industrial community, port-related businesses, agribusinesses, insurance companies, two of the area's three major hospitals, closely-held businesses and professional corporations, and real estate developers and developments.

Attorneys at Hunter, Maclean, Exley & Dunn are graduates of some of the nation's leading colleges, universities, and law schools. While earning their degrees, the firm's attorneys participated in a variety of academic and extracurricular activities and received honors, such as law review, moot court, Phi Beta Kappa, and Order of the Coif. Six attorneys hold advanced legal degrees, two are certified public accountants, three have master's degrees in business administration, and three have other master's degrees.

A VARIETY OF PRACTICE AREAS

Hunter, Maclean, Exley & Dunn offers a breadth and depth of experience to handle the full spectrum of legal issues that confront its clients. The firm regularly represents large organizations, including national and international manufacturing companies. Because of its longtime representation of two regional health care facilities, the firm has earned a reputation as one of Georgia's leading experts in the area of health care law. The firm's litigators handle a variety of matters ranging from personal injury cases to commercial litigation.

The firm is also heavily involved in all areas of commercial and business law. In addition to established corporations and other business entities, attorneys at the firm represent new and expanding businesses, assisting these entrepreneurial clients in corporate and partnership planning, acquisitions, and mergers. As the firm's business practice has grown, it has placed increasing emphasis on the areas of commercial leasing and finance, bankruptcy, securities law, and banking law. Hunter,

Maclean, Exley & Dunn's tax group, an expanding area of the firm's practice, routinely handles tax planning for individuals, partnerships, closely held corporations, and trusts and estates.

The firm's real estate attorneys recently handled all of the real property work in connection with the largest single industrial investment in Georgia's history. The

firm's real estate department frequently tackles complex financing, zoning, and environmental issues. Because of the increasing importance of environmental issues in real estate transactions, the firm has developed a generally recognized expertise in such environmental matters as the regulation of wetlands, hazardous waste storage, and underground storage tanks.

Hunter, Maclean, Exley & Dunn's admiralty lawyers handle all aspects of maritime law, including vessel documentation, cargo, personal injury and collision claims, charter property and other contract disputes, and U.S. Immigration, Customs, and Coast Guard administrative proceedings. In 1985, the admiralty group won a landmark case in the U.S. Court of Appeals for the Eleventh Circuit construing the constitutionality of the Supreme Court's admiralty rules.

The firm's 35,000-square-foot offices in downtown Savannah are fully wired for integrated, on-line computers in all offices. Its support staff of 60 employees includes paralegals, legal secretaries, and computer/word processing operators. With its diverse legal expertise, and technological and human resources, Hunter, Maclean, Exley & Dunn is prepared to serve its clients well into the next century.

With offices in historic downtown Savannah, Hunter, Maclean, Exley & Dunn is the largest law firm in Georgia outside Atlanta. *(Photo: Gabriel Benzur, Inc.)*

Savannah Electric and Power Company

As a company with headquarters at the hub of Savannah's historic district and as a member of the area's thriving economic and industrial community, Savannah Electric faces the unique task of looking backward and forward at the same time—backward to ensure that the community's historic heritage is preserved and promoted, and forward to ensure the continued vitality of the area through economic growth and development. In fulfilling this dual role, the company has sought to provide electric service that represents the latest in efficiency, but that is also compatible with the aesthetic and visual atmosphere of this rich historical area.

One notable example is the company's involvement in retrofitting downtown street lights with 19th century style "Bishop's crook" lamps. In cooperation with Historic Savannah Foundation, the Historic Improvements Team, and the City of Savannah, Savannah Electric is working to install replicas of these turn-of-the-century lights on four of the city's historic squares.

The company has also been required to respond to more immediate, practical lighting needs. Savannah's Showcase Neighborhood Project emphasizes enhanced lighting in high crime areas. In the first phase of this program, Savannah Electric upgraded 247 lights in one downtown district by converting existing lights from mercury vapor to high pressure sodium and increasing the wattage from 175 to 250.

PROMOTING GROWTH AND VITALITY IN SAVANNAH

Savannah Electric's role in the community includes a concern for the economic vitality of the area. As a member of the Savannah Economic Development

Authority, Savannah Electric takes an active role in promoting the area to new and expanding industries. In 1991, the Authority announced the completion of the Crossroads Business Center, a 1,784-acre business and industrial park located seven miles northwest of downtown Savannah. In the planning stages since 1986, this unique site was developed using the concept of pre-permitted "impact zones," which allow potential users to avoid the lengthy permitting process that generally precedes land acquisition. The Crossroads Business Center is the first of its kind in the nation and may well become a model for environmentally sensitive parks nationwide.

As a longtime corporate citizen of coastal Georgia, Savannah Electric and Power is proud of its role in contributing to the continued growth and vitality of Savannah and its sister communities.

Above: This scenic lake is an integral part of the Crossroads Business Center, the first business development site in the nation to apply the concept of pre-permitted "impact zones." Left: As part of the pre-permitting process, archaeologists conduct a survey at the Crossroads site.

Hilb, Rogal & Hamilton Company of Savannah

Blending years of insurance expertise with a nationwide reputation for personal service—and later adding a rapidly expanding American insurance agency system—has proven to be a recipe for success in Savannah. That ideal mix of ingredients first came together when Jones, Hill & Mercer, Inc. became Jones, Hill & Mercer Insurance Services and Jones Hill & Mercer Employee Benefits, Inc.

Both companies are now a division of Hilb, Rogal & Hamilton (HRH), whose offices in 20 states and the District of Columbia form a network of more than 50 agencies throughout the United States. Following the HRH merger in 1988, two other local independent agencies merged with the company, forming the largest single agency in the state of Georgia. Each member agency of the HRH network enjoys the expanded customer service of a large national firm while maintaining its autonomy through local management teams and meaningful community involvement.

COMPREHENSIVE INSURANCE AND EMPLOYEE BENEFITS SERVICES

With an emphasis on the Southeast Georgia market area, the agency provides all forms of personal and commercial risk management and insurance services for thousands of clients nationwide. While serving a diversity of business and professional service organizations, the company has been successful in marketing special programs for auto dealers, contractors, hotels and restaurants, the transportation industry, and municipalities. In addition, the firm offers a self-insured workers compensation claims administration division for large employers.

Jones, Hill & Mercer Employee Benefits has grown from a small department founded by Cecil Byers in 1969 to a separate company which now ranks in the top 1 percent of third party administration firms nationwide. Roger Holden, a 1968 University of Georgia graduate who joined the firm in 1982, states, "The company has been known as a pioneer in the business of writing and managing self-insured plans for employers." Based in Savannah, the firm provides coverage for thousands of local employees and their families with life insurance, short- and long-term disability, dental, cafeteria, and self-insured health plans. From small firms to Fortune 500 corporations, the company also serves businesses across the United States, including such diverse clients as banks, engineering companies, manufacturers, universities, utilities, and health care providers.

New clients of both the property/casualty and employee benefits divisions quickly discover what long-standing customers have always known: doing business with this 108-year-old Savannah company means much more than simply buying insurance. That fact is obvious to Chairman Emeritus Jack Jones Jr., whose father was an early partner in Jones & Hill. "It's our reputation for doing more for our customers and our insurance companies that has distinguished our agencies," he explains. "Going the extra mile has paid off for us because one of our principal sources of business is referrals from well-served clients."

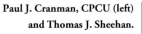

Paul J. Cranman, CPCU (left) and Thomas J. Sheehan.

STRENGTH THROUGH EXPERIENCE

One of HRH's largest agencies, the local office is the product of four successful mergers, beginning in 1981, which brought together decades of experience in the insurance industry. Today, both J. Clifford McCurry, CPCU, president of the property/casualty division, and W. Roger Holden, CLU, president of the employee benefits division, agree the mergers have provided tremendous advantages in terms of geographic distribution, shared expertise, and marketing strength.

The HRH story in Savannah begins with Jones & Hill Insurance, a local agency founded in 1885 as Haines & Rankin. As partners changed through the years, the business was renamed Jones & Hill after Jack M. Jones Sr. and Hugh Hill. Specializing in agri-chemical and fertilizer manufacturing and related business, Jones & Hill eventually became one of the largest privately owned, independent insurance agencies in the Southeast.

"The tremendous success of the Savannah port helped Jones & Hill extend service to 36 states," McCurry says. "We have insured cargo on ships that come into Savannah from throughout the nation and the world. We are ideally located to serve the shipping industry and related industries such as intermodal transportation."

The Mercer Insurance Agency, another predecessor of today's firms, was founded in 1902 by George A. Mercer. Like Jones & Hill, the Mercer agency grew and prospered during the first part of the 20th century. But in 1927, just before the stock market crash ushered in the Great Depression, a run by certificate holders forced Mercer into orderly liquidation. Johnny Mercer, the founder's son and Academy Award-winning lyricist of "Moon River" fame, came to the rescue of the certificate holders. With $250,000 of his own money, Mercer willingly bailed out the company, keeping a promise he once made to himself: "No one who ever believed in and bet on my father will ever lose a dime."

The Mercer Agency continued to grow under the leadership of Nick Mamalakis, who joined the firm in 1932 and later became president and chief executive officer. McCurry, who first worked at Mercer as a mail clerk, returned to the agency in 1971 after graduating from the University of Georgia. In 1981, when the firm merged with Jones & Hill, combined annual premium volume exceeded $15 million. The new firm—called Jones, Hill & Mercer—became one of the 100 largest agencies in the country. Risk management services included insurance brokerage and consulting, safety-loss control engineering, and self-insurance program design and administration, for which Jones, Hill & Mercer Employee Benefits is known as a pioneer.

Both Jones, Hill & Mercer Insurance Services and Jones, Hill & Mercer Employee Benefits joined HRH in 1988 as separate operating divisions. Two years later, Jones, Hill & Mercer Insurance Services merged with Dixon, Sheehan & Titus, a 35-year-old Savannah agency. That move created Jones, Hill, Mercer & Sheehan. The fourth merger occurred in 1991, when the firm joined forces with the 62-year-old Cranman Agency and became Jones, Hill, Mercer, Sheehan & Cranman.

"With these local agency mergers, our company name became almost as long as our tradition in Savannah," says McCurry. "We decided in 1992 to adopt our parent company name, and while we now operate as Hilb, Rogal & Hamilton Company of Savannah and Hilb, Rogal & Hamilton Employee Benefits, Inc., we will always be proud of the people who founded and built our agencies."

Roger Holden, CLU (left) and J. Cliff McCurry, CPCU.

"Our Strengths Are Yours"

The current size and extensive resources of the local offices contribute significantly to their ability to serve clients. But McCurry and Holden maintain that the strength of any company, no matter how large or small, is really determined by its employees. A combined staff of nearly 200 highly qualified professionals remains active in community affairs by serving on numerous boards in Savannah: United Way, Union Mission, and the Savannah Area Chamber of Commerce, among others. "For over 100 years, our company has encouraged active community involvement by our employees," McCurry says.

As the agencies approach the future, company officials have outlined one fundamental objective: to respond to the insurance needs of each client in a timely manner with risk management services that are on the cutting edge of new technology and trends, while exercising the highest level of pride and professional integrity.

"We pride ourselves on the work we do for our clients," Holden says. "We believe in performing services that will reduce costs for employers. When you do a quality job, it results in a less expensive product for the clients."

"Ours is a dynamic business with an exciting future," McCurry adds. "We take pride in caring for our customers, our insurance companies, our fellow employees, and our community. We strive daily to live up to our company motto 'Our Strengths Are Yours.'"

With an emphasis on the Southeast Georgia market area, the agency provides all forms of personal and commercial risk management and insurance services for thousands of clients nationwide.

1 8 8 6

1886
Strachan Shipping Co.

1887
NationsBank

1890
DeSoto Hilton Hotel

1890
Savannah State College

1893
Kennickell Printing Co.

1897
Oliver, Maner & Gray

In 1819, Moses Rogers served as captain and chief engineer of the *S.S. Savannah*, the first steamship to cross the Atlantic Ocean. This 1890 ship is being loaded with cotton and will be powered across the ocean by both steam and sail.

1 9 2 9

1899
South College

1909
Wachovia Bank of Georgia, N.A.

1917
Savannah Foods & Industries, Inc.

1918
The Branigar Organization, Inc.

1929
Savannah Technical Institute

The Central of Georgia Tybee train brought Savannahians to Tybee Island by the scores in the 1920s. Once there, the Tybrisa Pavilion seemed to offer something for everyone: a dance floor, band platform, bath house, suit and towel rentals, and a dining room. Later, there would even be bowling alleys and an arcade. For four glorious years, Tybrisa attracted the biggest swing bands of the time. Savannahians would linger until the final set, rushing madly to catch the midnight train back to the city. Tybrisa eventually began to decline, and fire wiped out the popular Tybee hangout in 1967.

Strachan Shipping Co.

In 1886, cotton was still king along Savannah's wharves. But trade in the bustling port had begun to diversify, with pine logs and barrels of pitch needing transport. Captain Frank Garden Strachan, a commodore of clipper ships and veteran of the China trade, and Captain George P. Walker, a young Savannah businessman who knew shippers, saw an opportunity in this diversification.

Founded that year with a handshake on the floor of Savannah's historic Cotton Exchange, Strachan and Company, Ships Agents and Stevedores, was born. The founders put an innovative twist on the centuries-old occupation of stevedoring by specializing as agents for

With over a century of experience as ships agents, Strachan has also owned its own vessels. The Georgia, circa 1929, was a Strachan vessel.

ship owners. Historically, a ship's owner, captain, or member of the crew took on the time-consuming responsibility of securing cargo for the vessel. As shipping became more diversified and complex, this specialty developed by Strachan and Walker was a welcome service in the U.S. shipping industry.

Captain Strachan acted as middleman, matching the shipper with the appropriate ship, and saw to it that the cargo was properly loaded. Captain Walker's job was to secure the right combination of cargo for particular vessels. The founders understood the elements of success: know the ships, know the shippers, and perform better than anyone else. More than a century later, those elements have not changed. Strachan Shipping Co. has become one of the industry's most dynamic, trusted ship agents and stevedores in the country.

CRYSTAL BALL GAZING

Considering the state of the shipping industry today, it seems that Captains Strachan and Walker must have had a crystal ball in hand when they decided to specialize. "We still follow the same principles on which we were founded," says J.R. Macpherson Jr., president of the company. "Our ability to give the shipper and steamship

lines we represent the best, most economical service possible is based on the very specialized, yet far-reaching knowledge our staff has concerning every aspect of the business. That, I believe, is what our founders had in mind."

What has changed, however, is the complexity of today's shipping industry. Explains Hank Dunn, vice president in charge of liner services, "With the advent of intermodalism in the late '60s—specifically, transferring cargo containers from one mode of transportation to another—and the larger, specialized ships that are more selective in their ports of call, the shipping world is much smaller and definitely more complex. We think Strachan has met these challenges better than anyone else."

Dunn points out that Strachan has 30 offices staffed with highly experienced, skilled personnel in all major ports and shipping centers in the United States. Computers give these offices immediate access to everything from a ship's manifest—an itemized list of cargo—to last minute schedule changes. "No matter what the cargo is, where it is, or where it's going, our staff will see that it gets there on time, on budget, and damage-free," Dunn says.

SERVING THE GLOBAL SHIPPING INDUSTRY

Handling more than 3,000 ship calls annually, Strachan represents shipping lines that go to virtually every port on the globe, from Europe to the Middle East to the Pacific Rim. The company is also closely tied with non-liner vessels that call on some out-of-the-way ports, like Pago Pago.

Strachan's stevedore operations can load and unload any cargo a ship can carry. Talmadge Glisson, local manager at the Savannah headquarters, recalls one unusual shipment. "Some fellows called and asked if we knew how to ship an electric generating plant, one large enough to run a small town, to Central America. We said 'sure.' Soon they showed up with some very bulky cargo. We handled it, and the shipment arrived safely."

Coordinating intermodal transportation, a substantial aspect of Strachan's operations at many ports throughout the United States, takes some very special skills and equipment. Bob Reid, vice president of the company's Atlanticargo Division in Charleston, South Carolina, explains the importance of Strachan's expertise at the Port of Charleston, where most cargo moves on some sort of intermodal basis. "Our specialized facilities and equipment for stuffing and stripping containers and our long-term relationships with truck and rail lines definitely give our customers the edge," he says.

"What it all boils down to is experience," adds Macpherson. "Every day Strachan is faced with new challenges, from types of cargo to changing shipping regulations. A great deal of the information and skills we need on a daily basis isn't found in any book. It comes from the accumulated knowledge of over a century of experience. I don't think anybody knows shipping like Strachan."

DeSoto Hilton Hotel

For more than a century, in the heart of the nation's largest registered historic district, the corner of Bull and Liberty streets has been the site of Savannah's grandest hotels. The DeSoto Hotel, built in 1890, reigned there for 76 years. Its successor was built on the site in 1966, and today, as the DeSoto Hilton Hotel, continues the tradition of elegance and superior service. Whether opening its doors for a meeting for hundreds of executives or welcoming a tourist set on seeing the sights of the city, the DeSoto Hilton offers guests the best in lodging and accommodations in Savannah.

A HOTEL WITH A HISTORY

The original DeSoto Hotel opened on the first day of 1890 amid gala New Year's Day festivities. The baroque Victorian structure provided a picture-perfect location for the frivolity that ushered in the Gay '90s. The six-floor, 300-room hotel was designed by William Preston of Boston and named for the Spanish explorer who in the early 16th century traveled through the region that would eventually become Georgia.

The old DeSoto was a legend in Savannah and across the South. Even today, longtime Savannah residents speak of the tenants who made the hotel their home for decades, and of the hotel "regulars" who relaxed on the veranda and became known as the Rocking Chair Brigade. The DeSoto was a social center of the city, with its grand ballrooms that introduced generations of debutantes to Savannah society.

The DeSoto even played a prominent role in local military lore. In 1898, General Fitzhugh Lee, nephew of Robert E. Lee, brought 15,000 men to Savannah en route to Cuba for the Spanish-American War. General Lee was ensconced at the DeSoto while his men were encamped at Forsyth Park and other areas. The ladies of the city, anxious to demonstrate Savannah hospitality, arranged to feed the general and all the soldiers, using the DeSoto as a central serving point.

The old-world charm served up by the DeSoto continued until the early 1960s when the grande dame of Savannah hospitality fell into disrepair. Restoration was economically and architecturally impossible, so the building was razed. In 1966, the new DeSoto Hotel was built and reopened on the same site. Just two years later, the property was acquired by the Hilton Corporation.

THE DESOTO TODAY

Over the years, the DeSoto Hilton and its predecessor have hosted some of the city's most distinguished guests, including five American presidents and celebrities and authors such as Sarah Bernhardt, Katherine Hepburn, Somerset Maugham, and Margaret Mitchell.

Celebrities and the not-so-famous today enter the 15-story hotel and automatically gaze upward at the spectacular crystal chandeliers in the DeSoto's luxuriously appointed lobby. The hotel has 250 guest rooms, each of which features a view of the city's historic district

Whether opening its doors for a meeting for hundreds of executives or welcoming a tourist set on seeing the sights of the city, the DeSoto Hilton offers guests the best in lodging and accommodations in Savannah.

and skyline. The elegant State Suite has been the choice of many dignitaries over the years, and on the second floor is a secluded outdoor swimming pool where guests can unwind and relax.

One of the city's largest hotels, the DeSoto Hilton can accommodate up to 350 people for conventions, seminars, and banquets. Ten meeting rooms offer a total of 20,000 square feet in meeting space. One of the most frequently requested meeting areas is the Harborview Room, located on the hotel's top floor. With wraparound floor-to-ceiling windows, the Harborview Room offers a breathtaking panorama of Savannah.

The hotel's restaurants and lounge are popular among hotel guests, as well as other visitors and Savannahians. The fabulous feasts served at the Pavilion restaurant and the casual meals available at Knickerbocker's Deli are unique in the city; in fact, dining at the DeSoto Hilton at Christmas and on other holidays is a tradition for many Savannahians. Live entertainment, refreshing drinks, and finger foods can be had at the hotel's well-known Red Lion Lounge.

The DeSoto Hilton, surrounded by history and steeped in its own, reigns as contemporary Savannah's grand hotel and meeting place. After more than a century, many believe the corner of Liberty and Bull streets remains the place to stay, dine, and be seen in Savannah.

Over the years, the DeSoto Hilton and its predecessor have hosted some of the city's most distinguished guests, including five American presidents.

NationsBank

An exciting chapter in banking history was written on December 31, 1991 with the merger of NCNB Corporation and C&S/Sovran. Operating banking offices in nine states and the District of Columbia, the new financial institution, NationsBank, is the fourth largest banking company in the United States with $113 billion in assets.

"Whether it's lending a hand to an event like the Olympics or considering a loan for a customer, NationsBank is dedicated to serving the communities where it operates," says Brian Foster, president of NationsBank/Savannah.

NationsBank has 14 branches in Savannah, the city where its Georgia predecessor was established over 85 years ago. In 1906, Mills B. Lane Sr., president of The Citizens Bank, spearheaded a merger with Southern Bank, forming Citizens & Southern Bank (C&S). His son, Mills B. Lane Jr., was also an innovative banker who served as president of C&S from 1946 to 1971.

Even today, the Lane family name remains synonymous with banking throughout the South and with philanthropic causes in Savannah. In his trademark low-key style, Mills Lane Jr. restored dozens of homes in downtown Savannah and donated millions of dollars to charities and other local organizations. That unique enthusiasm for community support is perpetuated at NationsBank through a variety of programs, including its role as the first corporate sponsor of the 1996 Atlanta Centennial Olympic Games.

According to Brian Foster, president of NationsBank/Savannah, such community spirit is typical of NationsBank. "Whether it's lending a hand to an event like the Olympics or considering a loan for a customer, NationsBank is dedicated to serving the communities where it operates," he says. "We have a decision-making process that is designed to serve our customers and the community at the local level."

That's why customer service—not geographic limits—is the driving force behind NationsBank. While most other bank holding companies organize their management teams within state boundaries, NationsBank's unique management structure is built around lines of business, which Foster believes results in faster, more efficient service. "We have been able to bring together those functions that can effectively be consolidated," he explains. "We then delegate authority to the lines of business in the cities and towns where we meet the customer."

COMPREHENSIVE CUSTOMER SERVICE

NationsBank operates more than 1,800 banking offices in Georgia, Florida, North Carolina, South Carolina, Virginia, Kentucky, Maryland, Tennessee, and Texas—a diverse, growing market area with a total population of 67 million people. Through the second largest branch network in America, NationsBank provides a full range of traditional banking products, such as checking accounts and certificates of deposit, to both retail and corporate customers.

Consumer and commercial services are grouped under NationsBank General Banking, which includes Community Banking, Consumer Banking, BankCard, Mortgage, Consumer Insurance, Retail Securities, and Dealer Finance. Among its major lines of business are Trust, Private Banking, the Secured Lending Group (Leasing, Commercial Finance, Factoring, and Real Estate Lending), Funds Management, Corporate Investments, and the asset management subsidiary, AMRESCO.

With an impressive 42 percent of the U.S. market share and annual revenues of more than $350 million, NationsBank is number one in the country in cash management. Its mortgage servicing division ranks sixth in the nation with $31 billion in mortgages. The trust department has $43 billion in assets under management, including small businesses and 1.8 million acres of farm land, timber stands, and ranches. Loans at NationsBank total $68 billion, while its consumer lending subsidiary—Financial Services—has 81,150 accounts and operates 110 offices throughout the United States. NationsBank customers have free access to the bank's 1,650 automatic teller machines and can use virtually all of the 80,000 ATMs throughout the country.

In addition to a concern for customer needs, NationsBank maintains an open corporate culture that encourages differing opinions, rewards individual achievement, and fosters teamwork. The bank also acknowledges its social responsibility to the communities it serves by revitalizing inner-city neighborhoods and businesses, helping local charities and organizations with financial assistance, or encouraging employees to donate a valuable resource—their time. Likewise, a nationally recognized employee benefits program offers workers flexibility in maintaining a healthy balance between responsibilities of the home and the workplace.

OVER A CENTURY OF INNOVATION IN SAVANNAH

NationsBank traces its roots in Savannah to the 1887 merger of Citizens Mutual Loan Company and The Citizens Bank of Savannah. A 1906 merger with Southern Bank created C&S, which quickly became the state's dominant bank. On December 14, 1907, the cornerstone was laid in Savannah for the Greco-Roman headquarters structure that would soon be known throughout the C&S system as "22 Bull Street." By the 1920s, the system had grown to include offices in Savannah, Augusta, Atlanta, and Macon.

In the 1920s and 1930s, many Georgia businesses and banks folded as the cotton farming industry fell victim to the boll weevil. Recognizing that dependence on only one crop was draining the land and sending farmers into bankruptcy, C&S encouraged alternative crops and the raising of livestock. Other agricultural development efforts supported by the bank included the nation's first irrigation equipment loans; research into the use of slash pine for papermaking, which led to the development of the timber industry; creation of model tobacco farms; and the importation of tank trucks to haul water to drought-parched cattle and fields.

Despite the financially difficult times, C&S forged ahead, acquiring even more banks throughout Georgia and opening its first South Carolina office in 1934. By 1939, on the brink of World War II, C&S deposits had reached $100 million. The bank was also building a reputation as a good place to work through a variety of company-paid benefits: Among the innovative programs started at C&S were group insurance (1926), profit sharing (1940), and pension plan benefits (1948).

In 1946, Mills Lane Jr. succeeded his father as president of the bank. The younger Lane was a marketing genius who in the 1950s led the Southeastern banking industry in one innovation after another. Drive-in banking, instant cash, the 24-hour depository, and bank credit cards all had their beginnings in the Southeast at C&S.

The 1960s brought additional acquisitions, office openings, and innovations in the mortgage, factoring, international, and investment areas. In 1970, C&S became Georgia's first bank to allow cash advances during non-banking hours. In 1971, it was the first bank in the nation to offer instant cash withdrawals through an automated teller machine. That year also marked the end of an era when Mills Lane Jr. retired as C&S president. "Let the fresh troops come in and begin to assume command," he said. Richard L. Kattel succeeded Lane and served as president until the late 1970s when Bennett A. Brown was handed the reins.

In December 1907, a crowd looked on as workers laid the cornerstone of the original Citizens & Southern building at 22 Bull Street in Savannah.

The national banking landscape changed dramatically in 1980 after Congress passed legislation lifting interest rate controls and deregulating checking and other demand deposit accounts. With the way opened for further innovation, C&S created a variety of new credit products and checking accounts to better serve its customers. In 1985, the banking industry was liberated even further when Congress approved interstate banking. Then, in September 1990, C&S merged with Sovran, and 16 months later C&S/Sovran merged with NCNB to form NationsBank.

With an eye toward the future, NationsBank adheres to a corporate philosophy that encourages teamwork and loyalty in a workplace where people care for each other and are committed to serving customers effectively. Those values echo the words of Mills B. Lane Jr. in *C&S The First 100 Years*, published in 1987. "My idea was simply to get people to begin regarding a bank as a friendly place," Lane said. "We're a department store for money, and it's our job to make people trust us, want to do business with us, and feel comfortable in our bank."

The Armstrong Plaza office, located on Savannah's southside, is one of 14 NationsBank branches in the city today.

Both in Savannah and across the region it serves, NationsBank and its predecessors have built a broad base of loyal customers who expect the finest in modern banking services. As it looks ahead to a new century, NationsBank is well-positioned with the power to make a difference in its communities.

Savannah State College

Located on a 165-acre campus graced with historic buildings and moss-draped oaks, Savannah State College has for more than a century made invaluable contributions to the educational, economic, and cultural life of the city and region.

The college was founded in 1890 as a department of the state university "for the education and training of Negro students." Originally named Georgia State Industrial College for Colored Youths, the college today is a senior residential unit of the University System of Georgia, whose mission embraces individuals regardless of race, ethnicity, or cultural heritage. Approximately 2,700 full-time students attend Savannah State, many of whom are residents of Georgia.

A HISTORY OF ACADEMIC EXCELLENCE

Savannah State awarded its first baccalaureate degree in 1898, and today continues to offer primarily undergraduate programs. Through its three major schools—The School of Business, The School of Humanities and Social Sciences, and The School of Sciences and Technology—the college offers B.A., B.S., and A.A. degrees in 36 majors. Among its extensive offerings are courses in accounting, information systems, management, marketing, English language and literature, music, criminal justice, history, political science, social work, sociology, chemistry, biology, marine biology, environmental studies, mathematics, civil engineering technology, mechanical engineering technology, chemical engineering technology, mass communications, computer science technology, and physics.

Since its founding, the college has continued to add new programs of study. Among the most recent additions are Advanced Water Technology, Teacher Certification Initiative, and the Hospitality Management Program.

Accredited by the Southern Association of Colleges and Schools, Savannah State College has 131 full-time faculty members, more than half of whom hold doctorate degrees. The college has also earned specialized accreditation in civil engineering technology, electronics engineering technology, mechanical engineering technology, computer engineering technology, and social work.

AN ACTIVE CAMPUS LIFE

Savannah State is proud of the fact that it provides a supportive, nurturing environment where students can not only explore myriad career options but also enjoy a full campus life. A large number of students live on campus in seven residence halls, and a variety of extracurricular activities promote socializing and the development of personal interests. Based on campus are more than 60 student organizations catering to such individual interests as athletics, fraternal organizations, scholarship, publications, community service, music, drama, and art.

Students in the mass communications department receive hands-on experience with state-of-the-art equipment in the department's television studios.

Football, basketball, baseball, tennis, and other sporting events also are popular pastimes for Savannah State students. The college is a member of the Southeastern Intercollegiate Athletic Conference and the National Collegiate Athletic Association, NCAA Division II.

In addition, Savannah State attracts many students because of its military training programs. On-campus Army and Naval ROTC programs allow students to prepare for commissioned service as regular or reserve officers in the Army, Army National Guard, Navy, or Marine Corps while they are attending college.

AN IMPORTANT IMPACT ON THE SAVANNAH COMMUNITY

Savannah State students also put their youthful energies to work outside the campus. Each year students, along with faculty and staff, assist thousands of Chatham County residents through public service and community projects such as Upward Bound, the Early Intervention Program, and the National Youth Sports Program. Many members of the college community also actively participate in and support agencies such as the United Way, the Savannah Symphony, the Coastal Jazz Society, Special Olympics, the Junior League of Savannah, the American Red Cross, Arthritis Foundation, Heart Association, the Chamber of Commerce, local museums, and private industry councils.

Since its beginning just before the turn of the century, the college has had a profound economic impact on the city. In 1990, Savannah State was responsible for more than $83 million in estimated expenditures in the Savannah area, an impressive figure which includes

salaries of college personnel, the purchase of supplies and materials for the college, grants acquired by the college, and student and college personnel spending.

Through the years, Savannah State has produced over 25,000 graduates who can effectively compete for jobs all over the country in business, industry, human services, communications, government, and the military. The college has also provided area business and industry with countless well-trained employees.

College officials say Savannah State is "committed to becoming an indispensable educational resource, not only for its multicultural and multiracial students corps, but also for the surrounding urban community and the entire region." As a historically black institution, Savannah State College is a unique community resource that helps interpret the cultural and historical legacy of black Americans throughout the coastal region of Georgia. Forging ahead into its second century of academic excellence, the college remains acutely aware that it must adjust to an ever-changing society and constantly seek ways to provide the necessary educational services to its constituencies.

A replica of the Blue Angels jet flown by Savannah State alumnus Lieutenant Commander Donnie Cochran was mounted for display on campus in 1991.

Hill Hall, constructed in 1901 by students and faculty in the industrial department, is the oldest standing building on the Savannah State campus.

Kennickell Printing Co.

For more than a century, Kennickell has built an exceptional reputation by combining old-fashioned values with exciting, fresh ideas.

Every hour of every day, more than 75 skilled craftsmen at Kennickell Printing Co. produce a variety of graphic communications products for a market that extends along the entire Eastern seaboard. At Kennickell, a team-like atmosphere and employee dedication are obvious to anyone who visits the company's bustling pressroom.

Each Kennickell employee takes pride in his or her responsibilities, a level of commitment which is crucial to a smooth, efficient production system. Simply put, everyone at Kennickell believes that printing is much more than an expensive wrapper or ornament; it is an essential element in heightening communication. Whether it's booklets, brochures, pamphlets, or other printed material, the company applies that philosophy to every creative product that comes off its presses.

BUILDING A NATIONAL CLIENT BASE SINCE 1892

As president of the long-established Savannah company, Al Kennickell is admittedly proud of the way the business has grown since his grandfather established the company in 1892. With an impressive client base and the most up-to-date equipment available, Kennickell is well on its way to being among the country's top printers.

No doubt, founder Milton Kennickell would be duly proud of the way his company is operating today. Already trained as a typesetter for the *Savannah Morning News*, Kennickell set out just before the turn of the century to start his own business in the heart of the city's historic district. Gradually, he built the company into a thriving printing business in anticipation of the day he would pass the reins on to his twin sons, Alfred and Ralph.

After graduating from Georgia Tech, the Kennickell twins returned to Savannah in 1932 to follow in their father's footsteps in the printing industry. Despite the difficult days of the Great Depression, the Kennickells managed to keep the company going at a steady pace and eventually moved the firm to larger facilities on President Street. Like most businesses throughout the country, Kennickell Printing experienced a growth spurt following World War II. During those years, five family members were involved in the day-to-day operations of the company.

Representing the third generation of Kennickells to run the business, Alfred's son, Al, graduated from The Citadel in 1977 and joined his cousin, Ralph Jr., at the company. In 1981, Al became president of Kennickell. Meanwhile, his cousin Ralph traveled to Washington, D.C. to oversee the U.S. government's printing operations.

Back in Savannah, Al began equipping the company with the latest in printing technology—an extensive inventory that includes two-, four-, and five-color presses, scanners, a top-notch pagination system, horizontal and vertical cameras, a color proofing system, die cutters, folders, an automatic pocket folder/gluer, and a saddle-

Kennickell strives to remain abreast of the latest in printing technology, from scanning and platemaking equipment, to printing and finishing operations.

stitch trimmer. Desktop publishing systems are also available for clients who use computers for layout and design. These additions, coupled with a commitment to cost-efficient service, boosted Kennickell's yearly sales from $1 million in the early 1980s to $6 million in 1987.

STATISTICAL PROCESS CONTROL

For more than a century, Kennickell has built an exceptional reputation by combining old-fashioned values with exciting, fresh ideas. A commitment to service, attention to detail, and an internal belief in teamwork complement new technology and such modern methods as Statistical Process Control (SPC).

The SPC philosophy in particular strikes an enthusiastic chord with Al Kennickell, who is looking forward to the firm's second century of helping customers in Savannah and across the nation with printing needs of all sizes. This bold, new course of action is a common-sense approach to business that revolves around teamwork and education. The result is continual improvement of products and service through employee education.

"You name it, and we do it," he says of the company's current array of services. "And with SPC there is no limit to how big we can be. The innovative ideas we are putting into place with SPC will separate us from the competition."

Kennickell first heard of SPC in the late 1980s, when colleagues in the Young Printing Presidents group were abuzz with the concept. "SPC is synonymous with the way the Japanese do business," he explains. "Actually it's the way America taught the Japanese to do business after World War II."

According to Kennickell, Japan has since fine-tuned the method, while America has let it slide, until recently.

SPC involves gathering statistics, studying them, and using them to improve business. For example, instead of constantly complaining about a secretary who has a problem with typographical errors in letters, an employee is encouraged to gather samples of the mistakes and offer suggestions as to how the co-worker can improve.

"Once you learn SPC, you understand it's the common-sense way to do business," Kennickell adds.

Evidence of the company's commitment to this unique method of employee education is Kennickell's on-site classroom in which a college professor teaches workers the how's and why's of SPC. "Because our employees understand the system, they are able to produce a better product," Kennickell says. "In that way, we are giving something of quality back to the community."

A GOOD NEIGHBOR IN SAVANNAH

Kennickell also believes in being a good neighbor in the Savannah area. As one of the few companies around with an environmentally safe press room, Kennickell is a friend to the earth, as well as its own employees. According to Lee Vanatta, sales manager for marketing and promotion, the company uses only non-toxic chemicals and soybean-based inks and varnishes. "As a result, we don't have barrels and barrels of hazardous materials to worry about hauling off," he explains.

With this commitment to the environment, a long-time dedication to service, and the latest technology in place, Kennickell is ready to enter its second century of business.

At Kennickell, a team-like atmosphere and employee dedication are obvious to anyone who visits the company's bustling pressroom.

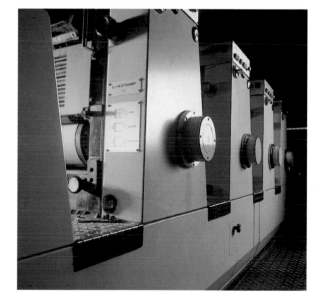

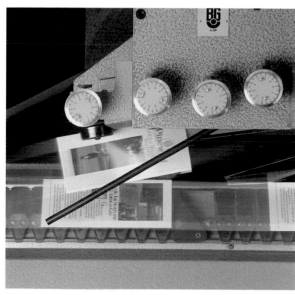

Oliver Maner & Gray

Since its beginnings nearly a century ago, the law firm of Oliver Maner & Gray has grown from a small partnership to a dynamic team of experienced and dedicated lawyers serving clients in a broad range of legal specialties. Although the firm's practice is concentrated primarily in Georgia, it has partners who are licensed to practice in North Carolina and South Carolina.

As one of the oldest law firms in Georgia, Oliver Maner & Gray holds the highest ratings granted by leading rating services for the legal profession. For example, one-third of the Savannah-area attorneys included in the 1991-92 edition of the *Best Lawyers in America* are partners of Oliver Maner & Gray.

Since its founding in 1897, Oliver Maner & Gray has grown from a small partnership to a dynamic team of experienced and dedicated lawyers.

DIVERSE LEGAL EXPERTISE

The firm, traditionally noted for its work in municipal finance and litigation, has grown to focus its legal practice in several additional areas, including public authorities and local governments, real estate and construction law, business law, taxation, and estate planning.

During the past 30 years, Oliver Maner & Gray has served as nationally recognized bond counsel for hundreds of tax-exempt municipal bond issues. The firm has represented issuers throughout the state of Georgia for all types of public facilities, including bonds for water and sewer facilities, courthouses, jails, electric generation and transmission facilities, resource recovery facilities, hospitals, schools, and housing projects.

In the field of public authorities and local governments, the firm works extensively with housing and industrial development authorities throughout Georgia. It also acts as counsel for local governments and constitutionally created authorities, and it represents municipalities and public employees in various litigation matters.

With respect to trial work, Oliver Maner & Gray has a large litigation division with extensive experience in state and federal trial courts. The firm has handled such matters as medical malpractice, white collar crime, insurance defense, products liability, admiralty, personal injury and wrongful death, general criminal and civil disputes, and commercial litigation.

The firm provides an array of services in the corporate area, ranging from the organization of small businesses and professional practices to public and private offerings of securities. Tax advice is rendered in connection with a large number of business transactions. The firm's corporate attorneys have structured liquidations, mergers, reorganizations, consolidations, and leveraged acquisitions. The firm also advises corporate clients in a variety of business and commercial endeavors, including employee compensation and benefit issues and the use of employee stock ownership plans to fund acquisitions.

The firm also engages extensively in the drafting of wills and trusts with emphasis on estate and gift tax planning. It handles probate matters, with particular emphasis on post-mortem tax planning. The tax partners are also very involved in the implementation of inter vivos trusts and generation-skipping planning techniques.

Oliver Maner & Gray's comprehensive real estate law practice covers the acquisition, construction, sale, and financing of industrial and commercial facilities, as well as the development of shopping centers, apartment complexes, and commercial and residential condominium projects. The firm has represented large general contractors, private construction companies, and material suppliers in the Savannah area.

SERVING SAVANNAH FOR NEARLY A CENTURY

Judge Hansford Dade Duncan Twiggs and Francis McDonald Oliver founded the firm in 1897 as Twiggs & Oliver. The firm's name changed several times over the years as its members died or retired. In 1955, Edwin Maner Jr. joined the partnership then headed by Joseph M. Oliver and known as Oliver, Davis & Maner. When Thomas S. Gray Jr. was named partner in 1967, the firm became Oliver Maner & Gray.

Since then, the firm has evolved into a partnership with 10 members and seven associates. The current partners in the firm are Thomas S. Gray Jr., William P. Franklin Jr., James L. Pannell, Julian R. Friedman, William T. Moore Jr., David H. Dickey, I. Gregory Hodges, Robert W. Schivera, Patrick T. O'Connor, and James P. Gerard. Charles L. Sparkman serves of counsel. With nearly a century-long heritage of legal expertise in Savannah, Oliver Maner & Gray will continue to build on the commitment made by its founders in 1897.

South College

In 1899, Dr. John Draughon took great pride in the graduates of his chain of business schools. That pride is still evident in Draughon's Savannah successor, South College. Over the years, South College has evolved into a multi-faceted, career-oriented institution whose graduates hold jobs in a variety of fields in Savannah and throughout the United States. Unlike the early Draughon's College, which offered a limited curriculum, South is an accredited two-year college that prides itself on staying abreast of changing times.

"As society and the business world have changed, so has South College," explains John T. South III, president. "We always have our eye on the future," he says. "A comprehensive strategic plan details a course of growth for this institution through 1998."

A PARTNER IN SAVANNAH

Members of the administration and faculty at South College are already doing tomorrow's homework by developing a close relationship with the Savannah business community. "We're constantly analyzing the needs of the community and responding by designing programs to meet those needs," South says.

With a faculty of more than 60 instructors—over 85 percent of whom hold advanced degrees—South College offers a variety of associate degrees: business administration, allied health, accounting, hotel and restaurant management, computer information systems, office administration, and paralegal studies. Certificates are available in several fields: administrative assistant, computerized accounting, legal accounting, legal secretary, medical assistant, medical transcription, micro-computer operator, and teaching paraprofessional.

With 12,000 square feet of classroom space, the school's downtown Savannah campus is housed today in two buildings on Whitaker Street just across from Forsyth Park. In 1980, a second facility was opened on a 4.5-acre campus amid the oaks and pines of Savannah's southside. The 13,000-square-foot brick building features modern classrooms, a 10,000-volume library, and a bookstore. Part of the college's strategic plan includes a two-story, 10,000-square-foot structure featuring a state-of-the-art computer lab and a new library, each of which will double the capacity of the present facilities. Also planned is a small auditorium which will be available for

community use. The college operates an additional campus in West Palm Beach, Florida, as well as affiliates in Montgomery, Alabama; Knoxville, Tennessee; Asheville, North Carolina; and St. Louis, Missouri.

A NEW DIRECTION

Around the turn of the century, the school was part of a network of 28 Draughon business colleges in 16 states. When John T. South Jr. acquired the Savannah branch in February 1975, the school had an enrollment of only 36 students. Under his leadership—and later that of his son, John T. South III—the college began to shift its emphasis from secretarial courses to a more traditional college curriculum. Though the institution was already accredited as a junior college by the Association of Independent Colleges and Schools, South recognized a need to reposition the college as a career-oriented institution. In 1986, its name was officially changed to South College.

For nearly 20 years, the Souths have made involvement in business and civic activities a priority. "We were anxious for our best and brightest young people to stay in Savannah after graduation," explains John South III. "We began an intensive hands-on recruitment effort, working with the chamber of commerce and the local business community. Those close relationships have helped us determine what jobs are available in Savannah."

A genuine concern for area young people is another important part of South College's action-oriented philosophy. The college participates in the chamber and public school district's Business Partnership program, which has paired South College with the Business, Legal and Financial Professions Academy at Savannah High School. Each year, the college also awards four scholarships to students recommended through the Youth Futures Authority, a communitywide effort that addresses the problems of at-risk youth.

It is this sort of investment that has allowed South College to expand from the limited focus of its early days—with classes in penmanship, punctuation, and business spelling—to today's comprehensive offerings. "As we prepare for the 21st century," says South, "we are committed to our standards and the changing needs of business in Savannah and throughout the region."

"We're constantly analyzing the needs of the community and responding by designing programs to meet those needs," says John T. South III, president.

Left: The South College logo welcomes students and visitors to the school's main campus on Savannah's southside.

Wachovia Bank of Georgia, N.A.

T he historic red brick building that stands on Wright Square has housed several venerable Savannah financial institutions during its distinguished 83-year banking history. Since 1977, it has served as the main office of the 12 Savannah branches of Wachovia Bank of Georgia, headquartered in Atlanta.

The historic red brick building that stands on Wright Square today houses the main Savannah office of Wachovia Bank of Georgia.

SERVING A DIVERSIFIED CUSTOMER BASE

From personal checking accounts to loan services to mortgage lending, Wachovia provides a wide range of banking services to thousands of Savannah area residents and businesses. The bank's 180 local employees are led by City President Eric Winger, who describes the bank as a "pillar of financial strength in a rapidly changing industry."

"Wachovia Bank of Georgia is well positioned to meet the challenges that are facing today's financial institutions," he says. "We have the people, services, technology, philosophy, and commitment to offer innovative services to meet the needs of all customers while maintaining credit quality."

According to Winger, the bank's goal is to serve its diversified customer base in the best manner possible. To accomplish this, Wachovia maintains three principal divisions: business banking, retail banking, and private banking. Business banking handles the complex needs of locally headquartered companies with annual revenues of $3 million or more. Retail banking for individuals and small businesses is offered at all 12 branches. A retail banking service Wachovia is particularly proud of is Personal Banking, a program in which each customer is assigned a Wachovia professional to handle all of his or her banking needs, from simple transactions to major loans. Finally, the private banking division serves individuals with substantial income and assets.

A PART OF SAVANNAH SINCE 1909

Wachovia's turn-of-the-century predecessor, Georgia State Savings & Loan, began the bank's tradition of serving customers from all income levels when it first opened in 1909. Sixty years later, in 1969, Georgia State was purchased by a shareholder of The First National Bank of Atlanta and for eight years operated as First Bank of Savannah. In 1977, First Bank was acquired by First Atlanta's parent company, First Atlanta Corp. One of First Atlanta's predecessor banks received the Southeast's first national bank charter in 1865.

In 1991, bank shareholders voted to rename the parent company Wachovia Corporation of Georgia, and First Atlanta became Wachovia Bank of Georgia, N.A. The new names reflect completion of the 1985 merger of First Atlanta Corporation and The Wachovia Corporation in North Carolina.

Wachovia is the anglicized form of the German word "Wachau," which means stream and meadowland. It was first used in America by 18th century European settlers to name a tract of land in North Carolina that reminded them of their homeland. An earlier group of these settlers served as missionaries to the Indians near Savannah in the 1730s.

As it has proven over the last 15 years in Savannah, Wachovia is committed to community outreach and philanthropy. Employees make significant contributions to the local quality of life by donating their time and talents to a myriad of nonprofit organizations, charities, and community improvement efforts. Wachovia professionals are frequently called on to speak about banking services or career opportunities at schools, universities, and civic groups. They serve on a variety of boards and committees and participate in road races, fund-raising walks, telethons, and many other charity events.

Likewise, the bank itself has made financial commitments to a number of public/private initiatives promoting community development. Wachovia is involved in both underwriting and purchasing bonds that finance housing, education, and municipal improvements. In addition, the bank facilitates the issuance and distribution of municipal bonds through its underwriting and marketing activities.

A long-standing commitment to the community has allowed Wachovia to accomplish a primary institutional objective "to fulfill responsibilities to communities, states, and the nation by promoting and contributing to economic and social progress, by giving to worthy charitable causes, and by participating in public interest activities."

Wachovia Bank of Georgia remains an important positive force in Savannah and throughout the state. A wide range of financial services, sound banking practices, dedicated teamwork, and a commitment to the community have made Wachovia a shining light in today's financial world.

Savannah Foods & Industries, Inc.

A sweet taste of the sun.

Those words are emblazoned on every bag of Dixie Crystals Sugar. As a slogan, it's straightforward, effective, and to the point. That's just the way Savannah Foods and Industries, Inc. wants it, because that's the way they have been making Dixie Crystals Sugar for 75 years now.

The company, founded in 1917, traces its humble roots to rural Louisiana. Savannah Foods has grown into a Fortune 500 company employing hundreds of workers, and is one of the nation's largest producers of refined cane and beet sugar.

From its corporate headquarters in historic downtown Savannah and its refinery in nearby Port Wentworth, Savannah Foods markets its products throughout the South under the familiar Dixie Crystals brand, as well as the Evercane, Colonial, and Pioneer labels and store brands. But corporate operations aren't restricted to Georgia. The company also operates cane-sugar refineries in Florida and Louisiana and sugar-beet processing plants in Michigan and Ohio.

THE REFINING PROCESS

Dixie Crystals Sugar is a familiar commodity to shoppers. But taking raw sugar and turning it into this well-known consumer staple is an intricate process.

Bulk raw cane sugar travels from the mills to the Port Wentworth refinery. Half of it is transported by rail from Florida. During the harvest season, "sugar trains" from the mills south of Lake Okeechobee deliver up to 30 cars per trip. The other half arrives by sea on barges from the Port of Palm Beach, Florida or from Central and South America, the Caribbean—even from India, the Philippines, and Australia. Huge cranes at the refinery's dock on the Savannah River unload the cargo, which is then weighed and stored in large warehouses.

The process of refining cane sugar is continuous, as byproducts of each step feed one another. The first step, called affination, combines the raw sugar with a hot syrup to form magma. The magma is loaded into an affination centrifugal, rotating at 1,200 rpm, for cleansing and to separate crystals from syrup. The crystals move on to the next step, while the syrup is pumped back for reuse.

The crystals are melted again into a liquid form to remove impurities and color. Milk of lime is added, and carbon dioxide is pumped through the mixture in four carbonization tanks, separating the impurities and about half of the color from the crystals.

The liquor is then pumped through filtering presses that allow only pure sucrose to move on. A final filtration

removes the remaining color, leaving a milky liquid that is processed for crystal formation.

THE HUMAN ELEMENT

This lengthy process is carried out by nearly 500 employees at the Port Wentworth refinery. No one appreciates their efforts more than W.W. Sprague, Savannah Foods president. "Even the most modern and efficient plant will not run effectively without a highly competent, well-trained, and motivated work force," he says.

Savannah Foods employees are encouraged to participate in corporate and community events, and they respond enthusiastically. Their high participation rate has been noted in such activities as Red Cross blood drives and United Way fund-raising efforts. "Our employees are really what sets the company apart," Sprague says.

THE PAST AND FUTURE

Savannah Foods traces its roots to the Adeline Sugar Factory in Jeanrette, Louisiana. Named for Sprague's great-grandmother, the factory was established in 1888, but fire destroyed it in 1913. That wasn't the end of disasters for the company: Floods and freezes caused more problems.

It was decided that the company's fortunes lay in a new location. In 1916, the firm and its 400 employees moved to a 30-acre tract of land on the Savannah River. On July 17, 1917, the Savannah Sugar Refining Corp., as the company was renamed, produced its first refined sugar at the new facility.

Seventy-five years later, as Savannah Foods & Industries Inc., the company looks to the foundation of its past while setting its sights on the future. That future is being protected with a companywide quality assurance program to ensure that Savannah Foods' high expectations are met with each product.

"In everything we do, we strive to get things right the first time," Sprague says. "We know the sugar business.

"We have many third-generation employees in our company who care deeply about the product they make. That's the difference at Savannah Foods."

Left: From its corporate headquarters in historic downtown Savannah and its refinery in nearby Port Wentworth, Savannah Foods markets its products throughout the South under the familiar Dixie Crystals brand.

The Branigar Organization, Inc.

Among moss-laden oaks, challenging golf courses, and picturesque salt marshes is a local treasure known as The Landings on Skidaway Island, a private, residential community developed by The Branigar Organization, Inc. of Savannah.

A subsidiary of Union Camp Corp. of Wayne, New Jersey, Branigar has developed and managed some of the most successful residential and resort properties in the United States. The Landings is no exception: since its inception, the project has received the Urban Land Institute Award for Excellence and *Southern Links* magazine's golf award for the "Best Combination of Courses."

Over the last 30 years, Branigar has been involved in community development and resort management in Wisconsin, Mississippi, and Florida, as well as Georgia.

Cecil Abarr, president of Branigar, describes the development as "day-to-day living with a dash of vacation and unmatched privacy." Encompassing over 4,400 acres, the development currently includes 2,400 single-family homes. With six golf courses, three tennis centers, three pools, three clubhouse facilities, and a fitness center, the member-owned Landings Club offers a variety of activities to families of all ages. The island also features two marinas and 40 miles of walking trails. Twenty-four-hour security is yet another benefit of life at The Landings.

Right: The Landings features six golf courses and two marinas.

Residents of the community, numbering about 5,000 at the end of 1991, are an interesting and versatile group: From 42 states and four foreign countries, they range from professionals and entrepreneurs to retirees. In addition, a growing number of residents are young Savannah families who have decided that the private community is a good place to raise children.

Branigar's development of The Landings has had a tremendous civic and economic impact on the Chatham County area. A recent Georgia Southern University study revealed that more that 70 percent of the Landings population is involved in cultural and charitable organizations. Donating more than 600,000 volunteer hours per year, these residents lend their time to a variety of projects in the community.

It is estimated that Landings residents pay more than $9.5 million in annual property taxes and $5 million in annual sales tax. Likewise, approximately $4 million in state income taxes are generated each year by residents. In a recent three-year period, residents spent more than $36 million on automobiles in the Savannah area, while the annual payroll of The Branigar Organization, Inc.

exceeded $10 million. Upon completion of the entire development, the appraised value of all Landings properties will approximate an impressive $1 billion.

BROAD EXPERIENCE IN RESIDENTIAL DEVELOPMENT

Founded in 1918 in Chicago as a family-owned real estate development company, The Branigar Organization, Inc. in its early years developed residential communities primarily in Chicago suburbs. In the late 1960s, the company was acquired by the Union Camp Corporation, and its headquarters was relocated to Savannah to develop Skidaway Island. The acquisition strengthened Branigar, allowing it to undertake other large projects. Over the last 30 years, Branigar has been involved in community development and resort management in Wisconsin, Mississippi, and Florida, as well as Georgia. With 1991 revenues of over $40 million, the company is now a major force not only in Savannah but also throughout the industry.

Branigar uses a team approach in the development of projects such as The Landings. The company has assembled experts in every area of real estate to ensure the success of its projects: marketing and sales, planning and design, financial control and analysis, horizontal and vertical development, and property management. In each new venture, Branigar puts to work its many corporate resources to stay on top of economic trends and fast-changing consumer dynamics.

According to Abarr, management of the company requires a constant balance of creativity and discipline. "We often need to develop unusual or creative approaches to development projects in order to breathe new life into a tough real estate market," he explains. "And we substantiate our approach with comprehensive financial analysis. This creative and entrepreneurial approach, combined with our corporate resources, gives Branigar an edge in real estate development and management."

Abarr also oversees the Branigar Credit Corp., which finances and services loans on consumer land purchases, and Transtates Properties, Inc., an affiliated organization that sells, leases, and manages commercial real estate.

A THOROUGH APPROACH TO EVERY PROJECT

The Branigar edge touted by Abarr is obvious in The Landings' master plan and the research that went into it. For example, planners limited the number of homes to be built and specified that almost half of the development be preserved as nature conservancies, parks, golf fairways, greenbelts, and trail systems. In the development phase, all factors affecting the property, including natural, cultural, political, economic, and regulatory conditions, were researched thoroughly. Likewise, a detailed design study was conducted for each element of the master plan—from the large-scale analysis of traffic circulation to the subtleties of street signs and mailboxes.

Branigar also established an Architectural Review Committee to ensure that all homes at The Landings would be constructed with the beauty of the setting in mind. For example, in an effort to preserve as many trees as possible, planners paid special attention to every tree more than six inches in diameter. The committee includes The Landings' architectural administrator, architects from the Savannah area, and residents of the development. This function is now managed by the Landings Association, an organization made up of Landings property owners. In addition, environmental specialists have helped guide the complicated course of compliance with regulations governing wetlands development and other similar issues.

The Branigar approach is well known throughout the United States. No two Branigar developments are alike, yet each is a recognizable product of the company's thorough research, expertise, and creativity. Indeed, the Savannah area benefits as both the headquarters for The Branigar Organization, Inc., and the site of one of its award-winning developments.

Above: All Branigar communities are designed and built with great environmental sensitivity. Left: Branigar-built facilities like the Plantation Clubhouse at The Landings are always of the highest quality.

Savannah Technical Institute

Savannah Tech is Accredited by the Southern Association of Colleges and Schools to award Associate Degrees and Diplomas.

When a business decides to open a new facility in Savannah, company officials often look to Savannah Technical Institute for assistance. Today, the institute plays a major role in the community's economic development by training employees of these new businesses. Likewise, Savannah Tech offers retraining programs for employees who are struggling to stay abreast of new technology.

Officials at Savannah Tech believe that the demand for worker retraining will be significant as the business community looks toward the year 2000. The institute has responded quickly to that need as part of its Total Quality Management program, which helps the administration remain focused on its customers, whether they are local business executives or traditional students. As Savannah Tech President Dr. Billy Hair says, "We're extremely customer-focused and responsive to the needs of the businesses in the communities we serve."

A LOCALLY GOVERNED INSTITUTION

Savannah Tech has been answering local educational and training needs since 1929 when it began as the Opportunity School sponsored by the Savannah Area Chamber of Commerce. Accredited by the Commission on Colleges of the Southern Association of Colleges and Schools to award Associate Degrees and Diplomas, Savannah Tech is today a division of the Savannah-

Chatham County Board of Public Education and the Georgia Department of Technical and Adult Education.

As a locally governed institution, Savannah Tech is able to make fast and informed responses to community requests and needs. For example, when the school needed a larger library to fulfill accreditation requirements, Savannah Tech turned to the Chatham County School Board. In 1990, the board agreed to raise funds for the library facility through a local $60 million bond referendum. Today, the state-of-the-art library, completed in 1992 on Savannah Tech's main campus, is proof of the advantages of the school's local orientation.

"Being locally governed allows us to remain close to our market and to respond faster to community needs," says Hair. "Out of 32 technical schools in the state, we're one of only four that are locally governed."

In 1982, when Dr. Hair recognized the need for a strong outside source of advice and funding from the business community, he approached the school board for permission to establish the Savannah Tech Foundation. Today, the institute receives financial and administrative assistance from this nonprofit, independent organization. In keeping with its mission to provide support and development of Savannah Tech's educational, cultural, social, civic, and professional endeavors, the Foundation helps draw the institute into the mainstream of Savannah's business and industrial environment. It also acquires and administers cash, grants, scholarships, and other funds and properties from individuals.

OVER 60 YEARS OF GROWTH IN SAVANNAH

Since the school opened more than 60 years ago, Savannah Tech's annual enrollment has grown to over 8,000 students at five locations that serve Chatham, Liberty, Bryan, and Effingham counties. More than 150

Ninety percent of Savannah Tech's graduates seek employment in Chatham and neighboring counties.

trained professionals are members of the Savannah Tech faculty and administration.

The school's contributions to the four-county area are evident at each of its campuses. In 1991, for example, more than 200 Fort Howard Corporation employees were trained at the West Chatham Technology Center. That facility assists new and existing industries with company audits, customized training, and education, as well as offering seminars and other training programs to the West Chatham area.

EastSide Tech, a partnership with the City of Savannah, offers short-term courses for entry-level employment to residents of local inner-city neighborhoods. These students can enroll in courses on a variety of subjects including nursing assistant, carpentry, lawn maintenance, and clerical aide.

The Liberty County Campus serves hundreds of military personnel, their dependents, and the community. During Operation Desert Storm more than 68 percent of the students attending the Fort Stewart Center were called to duty. Savannah Tech responded to the needs of their spouses who remained behind by offering short-term courses in office skills and health-related fields.

Savannah Tech's $9 million main campus, completed in 1981, offers more than 40 associate degree, diploma, and certificate programs. Savannah Tech provides educational, vocational, and specialized career training for those seeking entry-level positions in the work force, as well as individuals who want to improve their skills. Continuing education classes, seminars, and workshops aimed at enhancing existing skills or developing a career change are available at all campuses.

TRADITIONAL AND INNOVATIVE TRAINING PROGRAMS

Savannah Tech awards Associate Degrees in Accounting, Biomedical Engineering Technology, Civil Engineering Technology, Computer Programming, Electromechanical Engineering Technology, Electronics Engineering Technology, Fire Science, Marketing Management, and

The trucking industry frequently donates equipment to Savannah Tech's Commercial Truck Driving program, which in turn provides a steady pool of qualified drivers.

Secretarial Science. Diplomas are also awarded in allied health, business, industrial, technical, and service occupations. Courses range from Mechanical and Electrical Systems in the Automotive Collision Repair program to Techniques of Haircutting in the Cosmetology program.

New programs are regularly added to the Savannah Tech curriculum. The Brighter Future Program, currently in the pilot phase, is a unique joint enrollment program that gives at-risk high school students a new reason to strive for a diploma. Guidance counselors at area schools recommend and refer students who are several years older than peers in their grade level to take part in extracurricular vocational training on the Savannah Tech campus. Likewise, incoming Savannah Tech students may take advantage of developmental studies training which teaches basic education skills in English, math, and reading.

Another program that provides further evidence of Savannah Tech's versatility is its certificate program in Commercial Truck Driving. "This program is an excellent example of how we have responded to the community and created a partnership with area trucking companies," Hair says. "The companies were desperate for drivers and said they would give us the equipment if we would train the drivers."

But Savannah Tech is unique in another aspect: every graduate comes with a warranty. "If an employer who hires a Savannah Tech student feels like the student needs additional training, we will retrain him at no cost to the employer," Hair says. The Savannah Tech guarantee, which remains in effect for two years after graduation, applies to any graduate who is employed in the field of his or her training.

Like all of its programs, the Savannah Tech student warranty points to the school's confidence in its students and its commitment to the community. Through its long-time partnership with area business and industry to help train and retrain a legion of skilled workers, Savannah Technical Institute has positioned itself as an educational leader in southeast Georgia.

Left: Savannah Tech offers over 40 career choices, as well as continuing education courses, seminars, workshops, and teleconferences with flexible day and evening schedules.

LORI PARNELL HESTER

1 9 3 0

1935
Union Camp Corporation

1936
Roger Wood Foods, Inc.

1939
Blue Cross and Blue Shield of Georgia

1945
Georgia Ports Authority

1948
Stone Savannah River Pulp & Paper, Inc.

1954
The Coastal Bank

Cochran's Wood and Produce Company, located at 1501 West Broad Street, offered to 1934 shoppers "hot dogs, hamburger, fruit and vegetables," not to mention Atlas tires. It also offered convenience; the sign says, "We Never Close."

1 9 7 9

1955
Memorial Medical Center

1969
Effingham County Hospital

1970
Charter Hospital of Savannah

1971
Willingway Hospital

1976
J.T. Turner Construction Co., Inc.

1978
EM Industries, Inc.

1978
Gulfstream Aerospace Corporation

During its 34 months of operation, the Southeastern Shipbuilding Corporation built 88 of the Navy's more than 2,400 Liberty Ships, nicknamed "Ugly Ducklings." The ships were used to ferry cargo and soldiers during World War II and in the Vietnam War, but were dry-docked or scrapped in the 1960s and 1970s. The first one, built in 1942, was appropriately named *James Oglethorpe, Liberty Ship,* after Savannah's founder.

Union Camp Corporation

U nion Camp Corporation, headquartered in Wayne, New Jersey, is a worldwide company and a leading manufacturer of paper, packaging, chemicals, and building products. The largest of its facilities, and the largest paper manufacturing and converting operation of its kind in the world, is the company's Savannah complex. Providing over 3,600 local jobs, Union Camp's economic impact on the community is estimated at over a half-billion dollars annually.

DIVERSE MANUFACTURING OPERATIONS

The unique and massive Savannah complex, located on a 450-acre site with over 100 acres under roof, consists of four separate manufacturing operations: a pulp and paper mill, a corrugated box factory, a paper bag plant, and a chemical manufacturing plant. The company's Forest Resources Group (woodlands and building products), Corporate Engineering Division, Corporate Environmental Affairs, and Branigar Organization (wholly-owned land development subsidiary) are also headquartered locally.

A three-year, $475 million restructuring of the pulp and paper mill has elevated it to world-class status, reducing costs by 12 percent across the board and increasing production by 10 percent. With its new Number Eight paper machine capable of producing

almost a half-million tons of product per year, the rated capacity of the six-machine mill is now over 3,400 tons per day or 1.25 million tons annually.

Mill production ranges from the lightest weight unbleached paper used in the manufacture of paper bags to heavy duty linerboard used in the production of corrugated boxes. Additionally, one paper machine is dedicated almost exclusively to manufacturing saturating kraft, a sheet used as the core stock in making plastic laminates for such end uses as counter tops and furniture. Two-thirds of the mill's production supplies the company's own packaging plants. The remainder is sold on the open market to domestic customers or exported to customers around the world.

Savannah Box produces more than 4.5 million corrugated containers per year, of which 25 percent are wax-coated cartons for the poultry industry. Boxes are also manufactured for food and beverage products, textiles, chemical and soap products, furniture, fabricated metal products, and electrical and non-electrical machinery. As an adjunct to the box operation, the Ultra Graphics department, one of the company's latest innovations, produces pre-printed linerboard with high quality graphics not possible with conventional box-making techniques.

The Bag Plant, officially known as Retail Packaging, produces more than 14 million paper bags daily on 60 high-speed, fully automated bag machines. Over 600 rolls of paper, 75 percent of which come from the Savannah mill, are converted daily. Its products include grocery bags and sacks, merchandise bags for non-food stores, bags for fast-food outlets, specialty bags, bags for frozen food, and mailer bags. Approximately one-third of the bags are printed in one to four colors.

The high-tech control room of the new Number Eight machine is capable of producing almost a half-million tons of product per year.

JOSEPH BYRD

Union Camp was one of the first companies in the forest products industry to recover and market wood pulp-based chemicals. Its chemical refining facility in Savannah is one of the largest, most efficient in the world. Tall Oil, a by-product of the pulping process for paper making, is the raw material from which fatty acids, rosins, resins, and resinates are derived. Union Camp sells these upgraded, higher value chemicals for use in products such as inks, adhesives, coating lubricants, plasticizers, and cosmetics.

Southeastern woodlands provide the raw materials base for most of Union Camp's products. The company's Forest Resources Group is responsible for total woodlands holdings of about 1.7 million acres spread over six southeastern states. Approximately 1 million of these acres in Georgia, South Carolina, and Florida are managed from Savannah to ensure a continuing wood supply for the Savannah Mill and two lumber manufacturing operations in southeast Georgia. Union Camp's annual regeneration of 30,000 to 40,000 acres of land makes it one of the largest farmers in the region.

PULLING TOGETHER IN SAVANNAH

The economic potential of the South's pine forests was largely unrealized until the early 1930s. At that time, Union Bag and Paper Corporation began negotiations with the Savannah Industrial Committee to build a pulp and paper mill in the city. After a plan was agreed on, Alexander Calder, president of Union Bag, said, "It was plain from the outset that we needed Savannah and Savannah needed us. That is why this project cannot help but be a success if we continue to pull together."

Construction of the $4 million pulp and paper mill was begun in 1935. Since then, Union Bag has enjoyed tremendous growth while putting thousands to work in Savannah and the region. In 1956, the company became Union Camp Corporation when it merged with Camp Manufacturing, Inc.

Since its arrival in Savannah, the company has been committed to being a good corporate citizen. Alexander "Sox" Calder Jr., the founder's son and successor as chairman and CEO, described the relationship with the city as a "two-way street, which is the best kind. It works better. Everybody wins."

Over the years, Union Camp has made significant contributions to community organizations and efforts. For example, it is a top local contributor to the United Way and has been ranked as the number one team in the

nation in the manufacturing group division for its contributions to the March of Dimes. Likewise, Union Camp employees tutor at the adult education center, work with the hearing impaired, serve as Boy and Girl Scout leaders, and work with the Special Olympics. In 1989, company volunteers devoted long hours to repairing the damage in the aftermath of Hurricane Hugo. Whatever the need, the community knows that Union Camp will be there to help.

The company further expresses its commitment to the quality of life in the community by building and operating facilities that are compatible with the environment. Union Camp strives to maintain a balance between resource conservation, healthy air and water, and the important economic and social benefits that industrial activity can provide. Extensive capital investment in its Savannah operations for environmental improvements is just one measure of Union Camp's commitment. More significantly, the company has often surpassed government requirements in its efforts to be a responsible steward of the environment.

Union Camp extends its environmental commitment to the areas of forest resource management, wildlife protection, and water quality and conservation. In addition, the company complies with air quality regulations which are among the most stringent in the world, and strives to meet energy requirements in innovative ways. Union Camp has also taken steps to alleviate the solid waste problem by implementing bold new recycling programs.

For over half a century, Union Camp has remained a tremendous positive force in the city and the region. As a major contributor to regional industrial growth, Union Camp is committed to improvements in community life and to the preservation of the environment in which it has made its home.

Left: The Union Camp Savannah complex is located on a 450-acre site with over 100 acres under roof.

The Ultra Graphics department produces pre-printed linerboard with high quality graphics not possible with conventional box-making techniques.

Roger Wood Foods, Inc.

A Roger Wood employee removes racks of smoked sausage from state-of-the-art computerized processing/smoking ovens.

Roger Wood Foods, Inc. has been a highly successful family-operated company since its founding in 1936. As a thriving business ranked among the country's top 200 meat-processing companies, Roger Wood Foods plans to maintain the small-company flexibility that has allowed it to best serve its customers over the years. That degree of independence also has enabled the company to look for new markets for its products and branch out into other areas of the food industry while continuing to process fine quality meats.

A Growing Family Business

Three generations of the Wood family have owned and operated the company. In 1913, Roger Wood moved to Savannah from Manassas, Georgia to start his career with Armour and Company. After military service during World War I, Wood returned to Savannah in 1920 and joined the Cudahy Packing Co., working his way up to local manager of the Savannah branch.

Driven by an entrepreneurial spirit, Wood and Charles Robbins formed their own meat-packing business in 1936. Ten years later, Wood became the sole owner of the company and renamed it Roger Wood Packing Co. In 1989, the company changed its name again to Roger Wood Foods, Inc. to reflect the diversification of its product lines.

Wood served as the company's president until his death in 1952. At that time, his son, Cyrus Wood, and son-in-law, Joseph M. Solana Jr., assumed control. Twenty years later, Solana bought out Woods' share in the company and served as president until his death in 1989. The company is now managed by Solana's children. David Solana is president, and brothers Matt and Mark Solana serve as treasurer and secretary, respectively.

Expanding to New Markets

From left: David W. Solana, president, J. Matthew Solana III, senior vice president-sales and marketing, and Mark F. Solana, vice president-specialty products division, continue a longtime tradition of family ownership at Roger Wood Foods.

Today, Roger Wood products are sold to grocery stores throughout Georgia, South Carolina, North Carolina, Tennessee, Alabama, and Florida. The company's 200 workers process the various meats, including hot dogs, smoked sausages, and smoked meats, and package them for distribution at a 75,000-square-foot plant in west Savannah. The facilities at the 22-acre site include production warehouses, a spacious cooling area, and corporate offices.

"The company's main thrust is and will continue to be bringing value-oriented meat items and food to our customers," says David Solana, "but we look for opportunities in markets where the large companies are not focusing their attention."

To that end, the company began diversifying in the late 1980s. It bought the Old Savannah Spice Company, which today manufactures seafood seasoning blends at Roger Wood facilities. The products are sold regionally through grocery stores, gift shops, and mail order catalogs. Another facility has been purchased to process shrimp, crab, and other value-added seafood items for the retail and institutional markets.

The company's longtime commitment to stay abreast of the latest trends in the food industry remains strong in the 1990s. For example, Roger Wood recently began processing and supplying chicken, beef, and pork barbeque to food service distributors and national fast food chains. The company has also begun developing an innovative line of meats for health-conscious consumers.

Community Commitment

Today, Roger Wood Foods perpetuates a strong commitment to the community that its founder initiated nearly 60 years ago. The company is a regular contributor to food banks and soup kitchens in Savannah and Augusta. When Hurricane Hugo devastated parts of the South Carolina coast in 1989, top management and a number of company employees loaded trucks with meats and food and drove to several hard-hit communities to serve hot meals.

Each year on St. Patrick's Day, when the city's Historic District is overflowing with celebrants, Roger Wood Foods sponsors hot dog booths at three downtown churches. The money raised from the sale of the hot dogs is donated to the churches' youth groups. Because of Roger Wood's service to others, the company was named "Corporation of the Year" in 1990 by the Savannah chapter of the International Management Council, an affiliate of the YMCA.

Through energetic management and a dedicated work force, Roger Wood Foods is prepared to remain a leading supplier of quality food items and to continue in its role as one of Savannah's outstanding corporate citizens.

Blue Cross and Blue Shield of Georgia

Founded in 1939 with a $1,000 loan from Candler Hospital, Blue Cross and Blue Shield of Georgia's Savannah office began offering health insurance as the Savannah Hospital Services Association. Today, Candler and many other local businesses and individuals count themselves among the 1.3 million Blue Cross and Blue Shield customers in Georgia—more subscribers than are served by the next 25 largest insurers in the state combined.

Recent statistics further confirm Blue Cross and Blue Shield's standing as a financially stable, not-for-profit corporation. According to Regional Manager Bob Lingle, the organization's net income in 1991 was $17 million, and a surplus of $78.2 million was available to pay expenses. Lingle attributes the company's consistent success to a firm foundation of excellent service, a full range of health care products, and efficient management committed to promoting cost-saving measures that benefit customers.

COVERING A 34-COUNTY REGION

In Savannah and 34 neighboring counties, Blue Cross and Blue Shield of Georgia offers coverage through the Savannah office and branches in Brunswick, Waycross, and Dublin. "Our statewide offices help us maintain a closer contact with our customers and the communities we do business in," Lingle explains. "It's part of our commitment to local service. People want to be close to an office so they can get a quick response." Further promoting fast, efficient service is a state-of-the-art communications system that links the Savannah office to the Blue Cross and Blue Shield of Georgia headquarters in Atlanta, the company's operations center in Columbus, and filing systems at hospitals and physician offices statewide.

Products offered by Blue Cross and Blue Shield include traditional insurance coverage such as group and self-insured plans for businesses, managed care plans that help control health care costs, and individual products such as FLEXPLUS (offered to people under age 65) and 65PLUS (a Medicare supplement product for individuals).

"Being a managed care company simply means we keep an eye on health care costs," Lingle says. "We develop all of our products to give customers the highest value for their health care dollars."

Blue Cross and Blue Shield's array of managed care services includes a Participating Physician Program involving 9,400 doctors who file all claims and paperwork for patients and offer cost savings to customers; the Prudent Buyer Program designed to control hospital charges; and Preferred Care Georgia, a preferred provider organization of doctors and hospitals who have agreed to offer their services at lower fees to Blue Cross and Blue Shield customers and to adhere to cost-containment features. Through its variety of managed care programs, Blue Cross and Blue Shield of Georgia reduced health care costs for its customers by $117 million in 1991.

The company's strong relationships with Savannah can be traced to 1937, when the Atlanta Blue Cross Plan was created by an act of the Georgia General Assembly with the goal of offering prepaid hospital care. The company, originally known as the United Hospitals Services Association of Atlanta, got its start with a $50,000 loan from five local hospitals. The original Atlanta office was followed by the Savannah Plan in 1939 and the Columbus Plan in 1947. The Columbus and Savannah Plans merged in 1966 and joined the Atlanta Plan in 1985 to form Blue Cross and Blue Shield of Georgia.

Many Savannah residents associate Sam Ward with Blue Cross and Blue Shield of Georgia's Savannah offices. Ward retired in January 1992 after 23 years of service, but continues to sell group insurance policies for the company on a part-time basis. Bob Lingle was named regional manager of the Savannah region upon Ward's retirement.

PROMOTING "THE COMMUNITY SPIRIT"

Like its counterparts across the country, Blue Cross and Blue Shield of Georgia is a visible participant in community activities. Statewide, it sponsors numerous educational programs and offers generous financial support to nonprofit groups such as the U.S. Olympic Committee. Locally, the company sponsors fun-runs and walkathons for the March of Dimes and participates in annual activities such as the Brunswick Seafood Festival. "Our subscribers are our friends and neighbors," Lingle says. "We believe in the community spirit."

Superlatives can be applied to all aspects of Blue Cross and Blue Shield of Georgia, the state's oldest and largest health insurer. Since its founding more than 50 years ago, the company has established an excellent reputation for service, efficiency, and a comprehensive product line.

Top: "Our subscribers are our friends and neighbors," says Regional Manager Bob Lingle. "We believe in the community spirit." Bottom: Customer Service Representative Donna Harmon assists a subscriber in the Savannah office.

Georgia Ports Authority

O n nearly any given day, tourists and Savannahians can watch giant oceangoing vessels travel in and out of the Savannah harbor. Nudged by tiny tugboats, the massive ships make their way under the bridge that spans the Savannah River to dock at the two deepwater terminals operated by the Georgia Ports Authority.

This fascinating scene involving ships from every corner of the globe is reenacted almost daily at the 220-acre Ocean Terminal in downtown Savannah and the 856-acre Garden City Terminal about seven miles west of downtown. In 1991 alone, ships docking at the two terminals carried an impressive 6.4 million tons of cargo. The GPA facilities are equipped to handle goods arriving in several forms: containerized, such as electronics, household goods, and clothing; liquid or dry bulk, such as grain, minerals, and jet fuel; breakbulk items, such as kaolin clay, steel, and machinery; and roll on/roll off (ro/ro) goods, such as heavy equipment.

Located seven miles from downtown Savannah, the 856-acre Garden City Terminal makes a significant contribution to the area's economic well-being.

A STATEWIDE ECONOMIC IMPACT

Clearly, the Port of Savannah has had a major impact on local and state economies. Bustling activity at the two Savannah terminals has generated port-related jobs for approximately 58,000 people across Georgia.

During 1991, U.S. Customs officers collected more than $201 million at the Port of Savannah. Likewise, business through the ports of Savannah and Brunswick, as well as inland barge terminals at Bainbridge and Columbus, provided $189 million in state and local tax revenue. And the economic benefits generated by Georgia's ports continue to grow as new and existing ocean carriers link the state's trade to the global marketplace.

"Georgia's ports serve everyone in the state and beyond," explains George Nichols, executive director of the Georgia Ports Authority. "Without our ports, Georgia could not compete as effectively as a world leader in the export of forest products, kaolin clay, carpet, and other manufactured goods."

A major portion of those exports is handled at Garden City Terminal's CONTAINERPORT, a modern facility capable of moving containerized cargo quickly and efficiently. In just an hour's time, each of the nine CONTAINERPORT cranes can move up to 35 containers. All six CONTAINERPORT berths are contiguous along a two-mile waterfront allowing easy dockside stowage and quick transfer for intermodal shipment. Another of CONTAINERPORT's most attractive selling points is its more than 2 million square feet of versatile indoor space for warehousing, distribution, stuffing and stripping, assembly/breakdown, export packing, and fabricating.

Nearly 75 percent of the world's goods today are shipped via container. Due in part to the CONTAINERPORT facility, more than 3 million tons of containerized cargo were handled at the Port of Savannah in 1991. "The continuing, dynamic growth of container traffic at Savannah is indicative of Georgia's expanding role in international trade," says Nichols. "In fact, nearly 50 ocean carriers currently serve Northern Europe, the Mediterranean, the Middle East, Asia, Central and South America, Africa, and Australia from the Garden City and Ocean terminals."

Garden City Terminal also handles liquid and dry bulk cargoes, as well as conventional breakbulk and ro/ro cargoes. In 1990, the Port of Savannah received international notoriety when 11 military ships bound for Operation Desert Shield were loaded at Garden City Terminal. The Georgia Ports Authority discharged an additional 23 returning vessels and received military honors for a job well done. In all, about 255,000 tons of cargo were shipped through Savannah to support U.S. efforts in the Persian Gulf.

The Georgia Ports Authority's Ocean Terminal facility offers 220 acres of indoor and outdoor storage, with 15 warehouses and transit sheds backing up 10 berths. One container crane and four gantry cranes, including two with heavy-lift capability, accommodate a variety of materials such as steel coils from the Far East, lumber and paper products from Georgia, and jute and burlap for the carpet industry.

DISTRIBUTION WITH EASE

Thanks to a comprehensive distribution network, cargoes arriving in Savannah can be moved from the port efficiently via rail, truck, and air. As the farthest inland port on the East Coast—located due south of Cleveland, Ohio—Savannah is within a day's haul over rail or road to many important midwestern markets. Interstates 95 and 16 intersect in Savannah, providing direct routes to Atlanta, the South's premier distribution center. These highways are located only 6.5 miles from the CONTAINERPORT gate. Approximately 100 trucking companies currently serve the port.

CSX and Norfolk Southern Railroads also transport cargo from Savannah's terminals to nearby yards, and then to huge intermodal facilities in Atlanta. CONTAINERPORT's ship-to-rail capabilities are impressive: the facility can accommodate up to 165 railcars simultaneously in loading positions, thus eliminating the need for cargo movement by road. Two-day "double-stack" train service to the Gulf of Mexico and beyond also is available from Savannah.

The distribution potential of the Savannah area is so great that major companies such as Chiquita, Del Monte, Kawasaki, and Komatsu all maintain key operations at or near the port. Pier I Imports also has a $7 million complex within a mile of the port. By basing their distribution centers in Savannah, these firms shorten the route their merchandise must take from the coast to retail outlets.

The often-complicated process of moving cargo from one place to another is further simplified by the port's Electronic Data Interchange (EDI) system. Helping to speed the processing and release of cargo, the system was designed to reduce the amount of paperwork a shipper must complete, streamlining cargo clearance and speeding up the movement of freight. The system brings greater efficiency to all port customers, including shipping agents, brokers and forwarders, trucking lines, and stevedores.

NEARLY 50 YEARS OF PROGRESS

When the Georgia Ports Authority was established in 1945, the computers and the state-of-the-art distribution capabilities of today were merely a dream. The organization was created by an act of the Georgia state legislature to operate state-owned port facilities and encourage international trade through the state of Georgia.

Today, the Georgia Ports Authority is directed by a board appointed by the governor. The authority meets monthly to make financial decisions and set business policies pertaining to its facilities. Headquarters is located at Garden City Terminal, and U.S. trade development offices are maintained in Savannah, Brunswick, Atlanta, and New York, with overseas offices in Oslo, Athens, and Tokyo.

As the parade of ships continues in and out of Savannah, people onshore can see only the tip of the iceberg. The iceberg, in this case, is the enormous impact the Port of Savannah has locally and statewide in terms of tax revenues, employment opportunities, and economic growth. With its streamlined loading facilities and efficient electronic information systems, the Port of Savannah is prepared to remain a major port and an important distribution center for decades to come.

Stone Savannah River Pulp & Paper, Inc.

It is difficult to imagine how life's everyday activities could be managed without the simple corrugated box. Almost everything in a home or office—furnishings, clothing, groceries, appliances, equipment—was at some point stored or delivered in a corrugated box.

About 885 tons of linerboard (the inside and outside of the corrugated box) are manufactured daily at Stone Savannah River Pulp & Paper, Inc. Located on the banks of the Savannah River, the company also produces approximately 740 tons of bleached market pulp which is used in the production of ultra fine papers worldwide. With ship-loading docks right at its back door, the company is able to streamline and speed up delivery of its products to customers around the globe.

A SUBSIDIARY OF STONE CONTAINER CORPORATION

Stone Savannah is a subsidiary of Stone Container Corporation, headquartered in Chicago. Since its founding as a paper and box supplier in 1926, the parent company has become the largest producer of corrugated containers in the world. A Fortune 100 firm, Stone Container is also the world's largest user of recyclable fiber, an important ingredient in the box-making process. Stone Container Corporation, a global paper and packaging company with annual sales of approximately $6 billion, has over 200 manufacturing facilities and sales offices throughout North America, continental Europe, the United Kingdom, and the Far East.

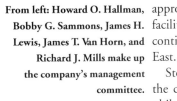

From left: Howard O. Hallman, Bobby G. Sammons, James H. Lewis, James T. Van Horn, and Richard J. Mills make up the company's management committee.

Stone Container is totally dedicated to excellence in the core business of pulp and paper. Through a simple philosophy of Innovation, Quality, and Service (IQS), the company puts the customer first in everything it does. To that end, Stone Container is committed to meeting its customers' needs by providing the most technically advanced packaging and containers (innovation), ensuring complete customer satisfaction by making the highest quality packaging and containers in the world (quality), and supplying products and services for customers when and where they want them (service). More than 32,000 talented Stone employees worldwide are wholly committed to the IQS philosophy.

DECADES OF PROGRESS IN SAVANNAH

Stone Savannah River Pulp & Paper had its beginnings in Savannah in the booming post-World War II years. The coastal city was just getting back on its feet, and the new pulp and paper mill, then called Southern Paperboard, provided a big boost to the local economy. Southern Paperboard started rolling in 1948 with a one-machine linerboard mill that produced 450 tons of linerboard material daily. After a name change in 1957, the company became known as the Robert Gair Paper Company. In the early 1960s, it was purchased by Continental Can. Finally, Stone Container Corporation purchased the company in 1983.

Since its founding, the Savannah plant has played a key role in the local economy. Today, its 510 employees continue a long-standing commitment to producing quality products. Like all Stone Container employees, the Savannah team adheres to the IQS philosophy. Under this innovative program, employees strive for excellence in everything they do—from product quality and customer satisfaction to community service. Stone employees display their enthusiastic civic pride in a variety of ways, whether it's coaching a little league baseball team, volunteering their talents for a charity event, or giving their time and money to the United Way.

Through the years, the company has undertaken several plant upgrades and expansions. These changes, aimed at improving working conditions, production techniques, and environmental sensitivity, have allowed Stone Savannah to remain competitive in the ever-changing paper industry. In 1989, a $346 million project modernized the linerboard facility and added equipment necessary to serve the growing bleached pulp market. Stone Savannah now produces up to 740 tons per day of the highest quality bleached pulp, which is sold for use in such products as printers' paper, fine writing paper, computer paper, frozen food packaging material, and magazine paper stock.

Stone also earmarked $40 million of the total project for an environmental improvement package. Equipment reflecting the most modern technical advances was installed to improve both water discharges and air emissions. A new system was also installed that will greatly reduce the emission of odorous gases from the mill. With state-of-the-art equipment, the non-condensable gases are collected and burned in the plant's lime kiln and power boiler, thus greatly reducing odor.

For decades, Stone Savannah River Pulp & Paper has produced the simple corrugated box in an efficient and environmentally sensitive way. Heading toward the 21st century, the company is proud to continue its longtime partnership with the people of Savannah.

Memorial Medical Center

Memorial Medical Center is an important part of Savannah's past, present, and future that has risen to new technological heights in the 1990s. Established in 1955, Memorial was the first to answer the growing city's need for specialized community health care. As a 250-bed general hospital opened as a memorial to Chatham County's World War II servicemen and women, Memorial pioneered a new era in medical services in coastal Georgia.

ADVANCED HEALTH CARE FOR SAVANNAH

From its earliest days, Memorial's mission has been to bring the most advanced health care to the community, eliminating the need for seriously ill patients to travel to Atlanta or Charleston for treatment.

The years since the mid-1950s have seen growth and change in the kinds of technologically advanced services the hospital provides. An important part of that growth today is Memorial's position at the center of Provident Health Services, Inc. As the parent company of a $250 million health care network, Provident is the third largest private employer in Chatham County.

Today's Memorial Medical Center is a sprawling 50-acre regional referral center for cancer care, trauma, poison control, high-risk obstetrics, neonatology, pediatrics, and cardiac care. Technology at Memorial has emerged in ways that not only make diagnoses easier for the physician, but also make hospital stays shorter and less costly for the patient.

In recent years, construction totaling millions of dollars has made Memorial the fastest growing medical facility in southeast Georgia. Ongoing construction and renovation have produced a state-of-the-art hospital that boasts approximately 530 beds and sophisticated tertiary care for the residents of 35 counties in southeast Georgia and southern South Carolina.

As part of its commitment to ongoing education, the Medical Center is associated with two of the most respected institutions in the state. Affiliated with the Medical College of Georgia and Mercer University School of Medicine, Memorial's Medical Education program shapes eager students into physicians and enables practicing physicians to be constantly updated on the latest advances in medical technology.

AN IMPRESSIVE SLATE OF MEDICAL SERVICES

Among the services unique to Memorial are on-site radiation therapy at the Savannah Regional Center for Cancer Care; Trauma Center I, the only Level I Trauma Center in southeast Georgia; LifeStar, the only hospital-based emergency helicopter service in the region; and the Heart Emergency Network, linking cardiac services at Memorial with member hospitals throughout the region. Memorial also recently opened The Children's Hospital, which offers services unique to southeast Georgia. The Children's Hospital has a pediatric intensive care unit and neonatal intensive care nurseries, one of five such units in the state. The "hospital within a hospital" also has a pediatric cardiology department and pharmacy.

The Medical Center's beautiful, modern Surgery Center opened in late 1991 and is considered one of the finest facilities of its kind in the Southeast. The center includes 19 operating rooms and features valet parking for patients, a computerized patient scheduling system, and top-of-the-line equipment.

Memorial also operates the Hyperbaric Oxygen Center, which uses pure oxygen chambers to promote healing of tissues and to fight infection; the Perinatal Center for high-risk expectant mothers; and Angel 3, a specially equipped ambulance for sick newborns.

Other services offered by Memorial include genetic counseling, infertility experts, on-site MRI (Magnetic Resonance Imaging) for diagnosing tumors and pinpointing internal injuries, pediatric rehabilitation, the Work Recovery Center, on-site kidney dialysis, lithotripsy at the Kidney Stone Center, and the Medical Education program, which trains not only new and practicing physicians but also nurses and other health professionals.

Equipment and technology are only part of what makes Memorial special. It is the hospital's physicians and staff—highly trained, caring professionals—who make a difference. Dedicated people and advanced technology: an unbeatable and absolutely essential combination in today's health care world.

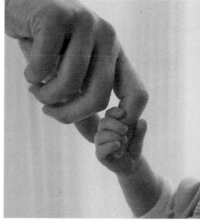

The Children's Hospital at Memorial includes one of only five neonatal intensive care nurseries in the state.

TIM RHOAD & ASSOCIATES, INC.

Left: Memorial's LifeStar is the only hospital-based emergency helicopter service in the region.

The Coastal Bank

When The Coastal Bank opened its first office in Hinesville, Georgia in 1954, it prided itself on being a friendly, hometown financial institution. As it has grown to include four offices in three counties, The Coastal Bank has strived to maintain that unmistakable down-home atmosphere by offering fast, convenient, courteous service. For nearly four decades, customers have demanded those qualities, and The Coastal Bank has always delivered.

SERVING SMALL AND MEDIUM-SIZED CUSTOMERS

Still headquartered in Hinesville, The Coastal Bank has evolved from a tiny bank with three employees into a thriving financial institution with $70 million in total assets. Its strong position in the financial world today sits well with bank President Charles Story.

"We service small and medium-sized businesses and professionals with loans of $200,000 to $500,000," Story says. "We're interested in small businesses that have the opportunity to grow so we can grow together."

Because of its expertise in handling smaller loans, The Coastal Bank is one of only four financial institutions in Georgia designated by the federal government as a "Preferred Lender" organization. According to Story, the Preferred Lender status allows the bank to handle Small Business Administration (SBA) loans.

"Many of our customers are owner-operated businesses," Story says of the numerous small companies Coastal has helped get off the ground. "Small Business Administration loans are just the kind of loans we're looking for. The program is perfect for us; we're not big enough to make really big loans, but we like it that way."

To help maintain the bank's long-time commitment to personal service, Story has assigned an experienced banking officer to coordinate the Preferred Lending program. An expert on every detail of the SBA loan process, the officer can help streamline the acquisition of a loan. "As a Preferred Lender, we greatly reduce the paperwork and red tape involved for each applicant," Story explains.

But The Coastal Bank offers much more than SBA loans. Thanks to its relatively small size, the bank's loan officers in all four branches take an individualized approach to every consumer and corporate loan. And because The Coastal Bank is locally owned, loan officers can make decisions immediately, which guarantees fast, convenient service for the customer.

Other services offered by The Coastal Bank include a variety of unique checking and savings accounts, certificates of deposit, individual retirement accounts, personal equity lines, overdraft protection, electronic funds transfer, direct deposit, safe deposit boxes, travelers cheques, cashier's checks, money orders, bank by mail, wire transfer, 24-hour banking, and automatic teller machines. The Coastal Bank is also a member of the Federal Deposit Insurance Corporation and the AVAIL, CIRRUS, and AFFN automatic teller machine networks.

GROWING WITH THE COASTAL REGION

The Coastal Bank has come a long way from its beginnings in Hinesville in the 1950s. Through the years, it has grown and prospered right along with the coastal region. In the early 1980s, the bank merged with Long State Bank and acquired its branch in Ludowici, Georgia. In 1986, The Coastal Bank bought Southern Bank and Trust Co. and began operating its three branches in Savannah. Two years later, the bank consolidated its two offices in downtown Savannah and moved them into a historic building on Johnson Square in the heart of Savannah's bustling financial district.

Today, The Coastal Bank perpetuates the philosophy of fast, convenient, and friendly service that has helped secure its strong financial standing throughout the coastal region.

Charles Story, president (left), and Bob Cassidy, executive vice president.

Right: Since 1988, The Coastal Bank has occupied this historic building in downtown Savannah.

"Love expressed by caring" is the staff motto at Effingham County Hospital, Extended Care Facility. This 45-bed hospital and 105-bed nursing home is located near Springfield, approximately 29 miles north of Savannah.

The hospital's 160-member staff is comprised primarily of Effingham County residents; as a result, the nurses, technicians, and other employees take pride in caring for their friends and neighbors. "We feel that the tender loving care of friends helping friends makes a difference at our facility," says Administrator Norma Morgan. "I like to think we have a family atmosphere at both the hospital and the nursing home."

SERVING EFFINGHAM COUNTY
Conveniently located in a single complex, the hospital and nursing home are situated on an 11-acre tract near the geographic center of the county on Georgia Highway 119. The facility opened in 1969 and became an affiliate of Candler Health Services, Inc., the parent organization of Savannah's Candler General Hospital, in 1986.

Morgan, who has been associated with the hospital since 1973 and has served as administrator since 1986, remembers the days before the hospital's existence when Effingham County residents had to drive nearly 30 miles for medical care. "The county had no hospital and only one doctor," she recalls. "Most people had to travel to Savannah for any kind of care."

Today, residents of Springfield, Rincon, Guyton, and other nearby towns need only travel a short distance to Effingham County Hospital. Accredited by the Joint Commission on Accreditation of Healthcare Organizations, the facility offers a long list of services, including acute and emergency care, radiology, ultrasound, CT scanning, mammography, stress testing, and respiratory, speech, physical, and occupational therapy. A complete laboratory and two operating rooms are also available.

In a typical year, the hospital and nursing home provide health services and long-term care for approximately 81,030 patients in Effingham County, an area designated by the Savannah Area Chamber of Commerce as "primed for growth." As a result, explains Morgan, offering quality care while growing with the county is the dual role the facility strives to play in the lives of local residents.

The 150 semi-private and private rooms in both the hospital and nursing home are spacious, colorful, and bright. In 1992, a second wing was added to the extended care facility, giving that section 49 additional long-term beds. Although the nursing home occupies its own wing in the complex, it is considered a "hospital-based" facility, offering a variety of benefits, including immediate access to physicians.

Effingham County Hospital

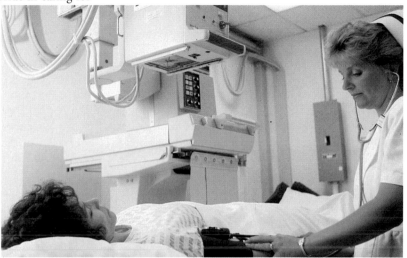

The nurses, technicians, and other employees at Effingham County Hospital take pride in caring for their friends and neighbors. *(Photo: Joseph Byrd)*

EXPERT CARE CLOSE TO HOME
Much has changed since the 1960s, when Effingham County had only one doctor and no health care facility. As the area has grown, so has the number of local health professionals. The county now boasts seven doctors and dentists, all of whom have been granted privileges at Effingham County Hospital. Their areas of expertise include family practice, anesthesiology, general surgery, internal medicine, pediatrics, and emergency room care. Another 10 Savannah-based physicians—family practitioners, neurologists, orthopedic surgeons, general surgeons, ENTs, urologists, and others—schedule office hours on a weekly basis at the hospital.

"This kind of relationship works well for the physicians and for us," Morgan says. "For example, the orthopedic surgeon and his partners are also team doctors for the Effingham County High School football team."

Likewise, the affiliation with Candler Health Services has proven to be a positive relationship for Effingham County Hospital. "Candler personnel are a source we can go to for information," says Morgan. "We are able to network with them for various services, like in-service education, that are difficult for smaller, rural hospitals to provide. Thanks to Candler, we've also been able to recruit more physicians. An affiliation like this is a model for the future; in order for rural hospitals to be successful, they have to attach themselves to their urban counterparts."

After more than 20 years of service, the staff of Effingham County Hospital remains dedicated to providing quality care close to home for all area residents. Says Morgan, "Love expressed by caring exemplifies our concern for others and our dedication to service."

Charter Hospital of Savannah

W hen people are faced with psychiatric or substance abuse problems, they often search for a retreat—a place where they can sort out their confusion and learn to cope with the difficulties of life. Many area residents find solace at Charter Hospital of Savannah, which offers treatment for children, teens, and adults.

"Our mission is to be the leading, most respected provider of quality mental health and addictive disease services in the Southeast," says Michael A. Zieman, Charter's administrator.

Charter's three-story, campus-like facility is nestled among tall Georgia pines on an eight-acre site near the center of Savannah. In addition to inpatient care, the 112-bed facility offers a full range of other services, including outpatient treatment, partial hospitalization programs, and specialty treatment programs for Co-Dependency, Post-Traumatic Stress Disorder, and Sexual Trauma.

Charter Hospital of Savannah is owned by Charter Medical Corporation of Macon, Georgia, which operates 96 psychiatric and medical/surgical facilities in the United States and abroad. In Savannah, a staff of over 200, including doctors, nurses, social workers, recreational and occupational therapists, alcohol and drug counselors, psychologists, and mental health professionals provide each patient with individualized quality care.

PSYCHIATRIC AND SUBSTANCE ABUSE TREATMENT

"Psychiatric and substance abuse problems are far more common than most people realize," says Michael A. Zieman, Charter's administrator. "They often are related to stress caused by family problems, divorce, unemployment, and performance in school or on the job. Consequently, mental illness and substance abuse can affect anyone, regardless of income level, educational background, gender, or age. With proper treatment, however, most patients can learn to cope with overwhelming pressures."

According to Zieman, individuals suffering from mental illness are often misunderstood. "They have the same needs, desires, and responses to others," he explains. "It is far more common for the mentally ill to display normal rather than abnormal behavior." Approximately one in 10 people who drink alcohol develops an addiction, and growing drug abuse is a national concern. Fortunately, Charter Hospital provides Savannah with a convenient, caring facility dedicated to treating a full range of psychiatric and substance abuse problems.

The Adult Addictive Disease Program, a specialty at Charter, combines medical evaluation, education, and rehabilitation. Upon admission, each patient undergoes a thorough medical examination and assessment. The detoxification process which follows lasts a minimum of 24 hours, but typically takes three to five days. During this step, skilled doctors and nurses assess the extent of the patient's disease and stabilize bodily functions. An individualized plan of care is developed and monitored throughout the patient's stay by the medical director and staff.

Recovery from alcohol and other drugs is a lifelong process. To assist in the initial and intensive recovery

Charter's campus-like facility is nestled among tall Georgia pines on an eight-acre sight near the center of Savannah.

process, the patient is assigned a counselor and becomes part of a unique fellowship and support system. Through education and assistance from the team, each patient takes with him an individualized plan of recovery that addresses the whole person and is free of mood-altering chemicals. The therapy program includes group therapy, education, recreational therapy, attendance at Alcoholics Anonymous or Narcotics Anonymous meetings, family sessions, and follow-up support.

Another specialty at Charter is the Adolescent Treatment Program, which provides care and treatment for 12- to 18-year-olds experiencing behavioral, emotional, or alcohol/drug related problems. Charter's program emphasizes the need for teenagers to meet problems head-on by accepting responsibility for their behavior and expressing emotions in an appropriate manner. In addition to an in-house school, the program offers individual, group, recreational, occupational, and family therapy.

GROWING TO MEET PATIENT NEEDS

Charter Hospital opened in 1967 on Waters Avenue as Broad Oaks Nursing Home. In 1972, Charter Medical Corporation purchased the facility and, at the request of a group of Savannah psychiatrists, converted it into a 72-bed psychiatric hospital serving mostly adults.

In 1984, the facility underwent an extensive renovation and added a 16-bed adolescent unit. In order to meet the needs of a growing city, Charter Medical Corporation purchased the present site in 1986 and constructed a state-of-the-art hospital to provide comprehensive psychiatric and substance abuse treatment for adults, adolescents, and children. The new facility, called Charter Hospital of Savannah, opened in October of 1987. Each of Charter's treatment units has a meeting

room and a patient lounge with a television, stereo, video cassette recorder, a patio area, and a small kitchen. The facility also has an outdoor swimming pool, tennis courts, picnic areas, and a gymnasium.

A member of the National Association of Private Psychiatric Hospitals, Charter operates in accordance with the standards of the Joint Commission on Accreditation of Healthcare Organizations. "Our mission is to be the leading, most respected provider of quality mental health and addictive disease services in the Southeast," says Zieman. "We want to provide a professional environment for employee growth and to promote personal commitment to excellence in a fiscally responsible manner."

With an outstanding professional staff providing the highest quality services, Charter Hospital of Savannah is dedicated to treating every patient with respect, courtesy, and dignity in a safe, confidential environment.

Above: A staff of over 200 professionals provide each patient with individualized quality care. Left: Each patient is assigned a counselor and becomes part of a unique fellowship and support system.

Willingway Hospital

Willingway's dedicated and caring staff have helped thousands with alcohol and drug problems.

Willingway Hospital, located in Statesboro, Georgia, about 50 miles northwest of Savannah, has treated more than 10,543 men, women, and teens addicted to alcohol or drugs since its founding in 1971. One of the oldest addiction treatment centers in the United States, Willingway Hospital also has a reputation for being one of the finest. In fact, Willingway was ranked among the top 20 hospitals in the United States in *The 100 Best Treatment Centers for Alcohol and Drug Abuse,* a book by John W. Wright and Linda Sunshine.

Founded by Dr. and Mrs. John Mooney, the hospital traces its beginnings to the early 1960s when the couple treated alcoholics in their Statesboro home. Today Willingway is a 40-bed facility on an 11-acre campus that has been intentionally kept small, secluded, and privately owned. Though John Mooney died in 1983, Mrs. Mooney and the couple's four children—Jimmy Mooney, Al Mooney, M.D., Carol Lind Bryan, and Bobby Mooney, M.D.—have remained involved in the hospital's daily operation.

In addition, Willingway's skilled team of 130 employees includes physicians who are board certified in addiction medicine, nurses, aides, and certified counselors. Through their own personal experiences, counselors on staff have first-hand knowledge of the disease, which enables them to truly share and provide support to new patients battling addiction. The high staff-to-patient ratio, about four to one, ensures an unsurpassed quality of care and fosters close relationships that aid in the recovery process.

COMPREHENSIVE, INDIVIDUALIZED TREATMENT

Willingway differs in several aspects from most alcohol and drug abuse treatment centers. At Willingway, drug or alcohol addiction is treated as a primary disease, one of the total person—body, soul, mind, and emotions.

Right: Tranquil surroundings allow patients to focus on recovery.

Treatment programs, which can last from four weeks to several months, are not predetermined by the type of addiction but vary according to severity and other circumstances particular to the individual. At Willingway, the daily routine and activities are less regimented than at many other treatment centers, and the hospital strives to maintain a relaxed and homelike atmosphere. Counselors are on duty from 9 a.m. to 11 p.m. every day and available 24 hours a day rather than solely by appointment.

Upon entering the hospital, the patient is placed under the closely monitored, around-the-clock care of the medical staff who assess the patient's condition and then supervise the detoxification process. The patient, upon stabilization, enters the second phase of treatment.

Although tailored to meet each patient's needs, the treatment program includes a "core" group of activities: individual, group, and family therapy under the supervision of the attending physician and guidance of a counselor; an educational program that includes the 12 Steps of Alcoholics Anonymous; classroom instruction and audio-visual presentations; discussion groups focusing on the steps to recovery; recreational therapy promoting healthy lifestyle changes; and supervised attendance at support group meetings. Because the support of the family is important to recovery, Willingway expects a family member to join the patient during the final five days of treatment. The hospital also operates a Family Center where other family members can stay free of charge.

Even after patients complete Willingway's residential program, the relationship with the hospital is maintained through the Continuing Care Program. An important part of this program is an individualized written plan which includes recommendations to the patient and his or her family members for maintaining a drug- and alcohol-free life for the patient. Willingway also has staff members available 24 hours a day at five regional offices in Georgia and Florida. These "coordinators" supervise weekly Continuing Care meetings for former patients and their families. The program also offers monthly "Adjusting to Living with Sobriety" workshops in Statesboro.

In addition, former patients become official members of Willingway's alumni organization which provides opportunities for sharing and socializing. The director of alumni relations coordinates regular group gatherings in host cities throughout the Southeast, and every spring Willingway stages a four-day homecoming weekend in Statesboro to reunite alumni and the Willingway staff. Former patients often travel thousands of miles to "come home" to the place where they first tasted sobriety.

As a caring partner and guide, Willingway has served alcoholics, addicts, and their families in need for over 20 years. With the longtime support and devotion of the Mooney family and an excellent hospital staff, Willingway is well-prepared to continue in its role as one of the best alcohol and drug treatment centers in the nation.

J.T. Turner Construction Co., Inc.

Founded in 1976 by Jim Turner, the J.T. Turner Construction Co., Inc. has established a reputation for fine work in several major areas of construction: commercial, residential, restoration, insurance repairs, and preservation. It is, however, the company's successful efforts at reviving the exteriors and interiors of some of the Historic District's most noteworthy homes and office buildings that have brought acclaim to the Savannah company—and truly captured Jim Turner's interest.

Turner started the company with the idea of doing primarily new residential and commercial construction, but just two years into his new venture, the "restoration bug" bit. "I had the opportunity to expand into the downtown area in 1978," says Turner. "Over the years, working on historic buildings has become the company's niche."

Turner's education and experience prepared him well for running his own business. A Thomasville, Georgia native, Turner graduated in 1973 with a bachelor of arts degree from Mercer University in Macon, Georgia, learned the financial aspects of running a business through a position with a bank, and then worked for several construction contractors to thoroughly learn the business.

Under Turner's leadership, the company has gained an excellent reputation for all types of construction work through quality craftsmanship, timeliness, and the dedication of its work crew. The firm's 10 project managers work closely with architects, subcontractors, and suppliers to ensure that building projects or repairs are completed on schedule and that the workmanship will fulfill clients' expectations. In addition, the experienced work crew considers each new project a challenge and tackles it with enthusiasm.

REMAKING HISTORY IN SAVANNAH

Restoring and preserving historic buildings was challenging and a bit daunting at first for the company, but through experience Turner and his project managers have come up with innovative and proven procedures to help guide the exacting and demanding work.

When starting a preservation job, Turner and a project manager research the history of the structure to find out

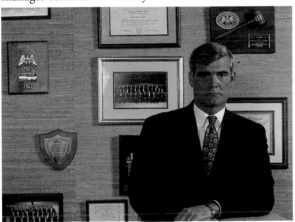

exactly how it was constructed and what it looked like, inside and out, at the time the building was completed. That task often involves working closely with the Historic Savannah Foundation, the Georgia Historical Society, and other area historic preservationists.

One recently completed preservation project was the Frederick Ball House at the corner of York and Habersham streets. "That was a true preservation project, because everything—the walls, floors, mantels, molding—is now circa 1810," Turner says.

In contrast, a restoration project involves restoring the exterior of the building to its original appearance, while the interior is often remodeled for modern use and convenience. The J.T. Turner Construction Co. restored the exterior of a 15,000-square-foot, three story warehouse at 218 W. State Street and converted the interior to offices for a local law firm. An elevator was installed, eight-foot mahogany doors were hung for an appropriate entrance, and a dropped ceiling was added to preserve the original plaster ceiling and hide unsightly phone lines and computer wires.

In all its projects, the company's attention to detail, careful coordination, and quality workmanship have been duly recognized. The firm has received several awards from the Historic Savannah Foundation for architectural preservation.

While the company's presence in downtown Savannah is noteworthy, many examples of Turner's work, both residential and commercial, can be seen throughout the city. The firm's portfolio includes custom homes built in a variety of styles, from the casual low country to the stately Georgian. J.T. Turner Construction has built supermarkets, doctors' offices, churches, shopping centers, and homes in private residential communities, such as The Landings on Skidaway Island. The company also rebuilt the historic Isle of Hope United Methodist Church (c. 1860) after it burned in 1984.

Fast and efficient insurance repairs are yet another specialty of J.T. Turner Construction Co. A 24-hour answering service and a mobile-phone network enable work crews, which are available seven days a week, to start repairs immediately. Through the years, the company has also established good working relationships with numerous insurance companies, agents, and claims adjusters.

For more than a decade, Turner and his company, through their work and voluntary community involvement, have made their mark on life in Savannah. The city and many of its finest buildings are much better off because of it.

Before and after photographs of the Frederick Ball House at the corner of York and Habersham streets showcase Turner's well-established preservation expertise.

Left: "Over the years, working on historic buildings has become the company's niche," says Jim Turner, founder of the company.

Gulfstream Aerospace Corporation

The Gulfstream IV, a marvel of business travel, can fly nonstop between continents thousands of miles apart.

For decades, the name Gulfstream has been synonymous with the world's finest and fastest business jets. Leaders of major corporations worldwide, as well as presidents and kings, fly Gulfstreams—and for obvious reasons. With nearly 250 square feet of cabin space, the newest Gulfstream jets can seat 16 to 19 people comfortably, cruise at speeds in excess of 525 miles per hour, and make nonstop flights of almost 5,000 miles in only nine hours.

These magnificent flying machines are manufactured in Savannah at Gulfstream Aerospace Corporation, headquarters of the Fortune 500 company established in 1978 by Allen E. Paulson. For nearly 15 years, he served as president, chairman, and chief executive officer until William C. Lowe came on board as president and CEO in 1992. Paulson plans to remain chairman of the company until his retirement.

His motto, "make it as perfect as you can," has become a challenge met head-on by 5,000 Gulfstream employees every day. Gulfstream President Bill Lowe says, "We focus on quality every day in many ways, including ongoing classes on improvement for everybody from the top on down." A huge banner displayed across the outside wall of the Gulfstream plant in Savannah touts QIP (Quality in Performance), a management and work strategy that all employees put to use in building the ultimate corporate aircraft.

The jobs performed by the 3,500 men and women at Gulfstream in Savannah run the gamut from plumbers and hand-tool leather workers to office personnel and electronic engineers. Chatham County's largest employer, Gulfstream occupies a 1.7 million-square-foot corporate office and manufacturing facility at the Savannah International Airport. The company also operates a smaller production facility, Gulfstream Aerospace Technologies, in Oklahoma City, Oklahoma and a completion service center in Long Beach, California.

Currently, approximately 120 Gulfstream models are in use by 32 governments across the globe. Seventeen C-20 series versions of the Gulfstream III are used by the U.S. Air Force and other U.S. military organizations. Many are part of the Special Air Missions (SAM) fleet used by the office of the U.S. President, the First Family, members of the President's cabinet, and other high-ranking government officials.

SETTING WORLD RECORDS

Today, the corporation is concentrating its marketing and production energies on the Gulfstream IV, the newest in a series of aircraft designed according to a philosophy of superiority in performance, cabin size and comfort, product quality, systems advancements, and reliability. The Gulfstream IV, a marvel of business travel, can fly nonstop between continents thousands of miles apart. The aircraft can also make stops at several airports in a single day without refueling. The Gulfstream IV has proven its superior performance and dependability by setting two historic around-the-world speed records.

The first record was established on June 12, 1987, when a crew including Paulson and three co-captains flew a standard Gulfstream IV west from Paris, France around the world. Sanctioned by the National Aeronautic Association and the Federal Aeronautique Internationale, the flight was the first in history to set world speed records while flying westbound instead of the more common eastbound routes. When the aircraft landed 45 hours, 25 minutes, and 10 seconds later, it had set two world records for circumnavigation of the earth and 22 records for speed between cities. Only four en route stops were made on the 22,886-mile journey. Average speed, including time on the ground, was 503.58 miles per hour.

Less than a year later, in February 1988, another Gulfstream IV broke the eastbound around-the-world speed record in a 23,048-mile journey from Houston, Texas, with Paulson as captain. Making only four stops, the aircraft averaged 637.71 miles per hour and made the trip in 36 hours, eight minutes.

SPACIOUS COMFORT, RELIABLE SERVICE

At a more common cruising speed of 525 miles per hour, Gulfstream IV offers a smooth, comfortable ride for passengers. Its 45-foot-long cabin with more than six feet of stand-up headroom is the largest of any aircraft designed for executive travel.

Approximately the size of a typical executive office, the Gulfstream cabin can accommodate a variety of seating arrangements, from individual workstations and conference areas to groupings set apart for relaxation. Sofas, fold-out seating, and actual beds are available for passengers who want to sleep on long distance trips. A large, walk-in baggage compartment, designed to hold 2,000 pounds of luggage and cargo, is located at the rear of the cabin. The jet's generous power supply allows passengers to operate a variety of electronic devices, including satellite communications equipment, Telex, facsimile machines, typewriters, computers, audio and visual systems, and small refrigerators.

Unlike most aircraft, which have cockpits equipped with a complex array of dials and gauges, the Gulfstream IV features six large cathode ray tube screens that display flight information and other statistics clearly in the form of visual commands, color cues, and other symbols generated by on-board air data computers. Supporting these electronic displays is a full complement of state-of-the-art avionics equipment, all installed during production, including accurate and reliable laser-driven inertial reference systems, radio altimeters, and flight guidance, navigation, and fault warning performance computers. The Gulfstream IV is powered by the Rolls-Royce Tay, a new generation turbofan engine with 27,700 pounds of available thrust.

The aircraft is supported around the clock by the Gulfstream Service Center and Product Support facilities located in Savannah and Long Beach. The company employs a team of maintenance professionals who are specially trained to work on Gulfstream aircraft. Likewise, a staff of engineering, design, and technical personnel are available for consultation on special

Approximately the size of a typical executive office, the Gulfstream cabin can accommodate a variety of seating arrangements, from individual workstations and conference areas to groupings set apart for relaxation.

problems relating to service, modification, and outfitting. On-site support and technical assistance is provided by a network of Gulfstream Technical Service representatives strategically positioned in the United States and abroad.

Parts and components can be delivered anywhere in the world within 24 hours, shipped directly from a Gulfstream Service Center in the United States or from an authorized center in Europe. The company also offers an exchange/rental program that enables operators to acquire needed parts or components quickly and at a reasonable cost.

The Gulfstream Learning Center, operated by FlightSafety International, provides initial instruction and subsequent retraining for flight crews and maintenance personnel. Located adjacent to the corporate headquarters in Savannah, this facility houses a Gulfstream IV digital/visual simulator, as well as simulators for other Gulfstream models.

ACHIEVEMENT IN THE AEROSPACE INDUSTRY

Although the Savannah company was not established until 1978, the first in a series of Gulfstream jets came into being in 1959. That year, the Grumman Corporation of Bethpage, Long Island, New York introduced the Gulfstream I, a large, twin-engine propjet and the first aircraft of its type and size designed specifically for business use. Many of the 201 Gulfstream I models produced are still operated today by their original owners.

The Gulfstream II made its debut in 1966 as a corporate jet capable of carrying 14 to 16 passengers, plus crew, for long distances at speeds well above other civilian jet aircraft. Some 256 Gulfstream II models were produced and delivered to corporations and government agencies in the United States and abroad. Even today, the National Aeronautics and Space Administration (NASA) uses a fleet of specially modified Gulfstream II planes to train astronauts in the space shuttle program.

The Gulfstream series arrived in Savannah in 1967

"We focus on quality every day in many ways, including ongoing classes on improvement for everybody from the top on down," says Bill Lowe, Gulfstream president.

The cockpit features six screens that display flight information and other statistics clearly in the form of visual commands, color cues, and other symbols.

when Grumman opened an assembly plant in west Chatham County. By 1978, the Gulfstream III—a larger corporate jet with increased thrust and range—was being developed. The new model was the first business aircraft to establish back-to-back speed records for eastbound around-the-world travel and for a continuous flight over both poles. Three Gulfstream III jets purchased by the Royal Danish Air Force were specially equipped to perform high altitude surveillance, air/sea rescue, medical-evacuation, and VIP transport missions. When the company ceased production of the Gulfstream III in January 1987, 202 jets had been delivered worldwide.

The Grumman facilities and programs were acquired in 1978 by Paulson, who has received a variety of awards for his achievements in the aerospace industry, including the prestigious Wright Brothers Trophy and the Horatio Alger Award. He is also an active member of the Society of Experimental Test Pilots. Under Paulson's leadership, the newly created Gulfstream Aerospace Corporation accelerated development of new models, and efforts were made to update and streamline the production process. To that end, modern production equipment was added to the subassembly system and the manufacture of thousands of vendor-supplied parts was brought in-house.

Right: With nearly 250 square feet of cabin space, the Gulfstream IV can cruise at speeds in excess of 525 miles per hour.

The company's latest model, Gulfstream IV, made its first test flight in 1985 and was certified by the FAA in 1987. But even before the first planes were delivered to customers in 1987, the aircraft had become the most desired business jet on the market, accumulating a sales backlog of more than 100 orders during a two-year period. On average, the Savannah facility now produces 31 Gulfstream IV aircraft every year.

Under a money-saving program called "New Again," Gulfstream also sells previously owned models at substantial discounts to businesses, military organizations, and governments. Each used jet acquired by the corporation undergoes a complete overhaul and is given a warranty that protects the plane for nearly as long as a new model. Like all of Gulfstream's personnel, employees in the "New Again" program remember Paulson's tireless work ethic, "make it as perfect as you can."

PURSUIT OF PERFECTION

In both business and civic affairs, Paulson leads by example, giving generously to the community where his employees make their homes. In 1987, he donated funds for the construction of Chatham County's newest state-of-the-art softball complex, tentatively chosen as the site of the 1996 Olympic softball tournaments. In Statesboro, some 50 miles northwest of Savannah, the Georgia Southern University championship football team plays its home games in the Allen E. Paulson stadium, a facility made possible by Paulson's generosity. Gulfstream has also endowed an engineering chair at Georgia Southern. Among the many local organizations supported by the company are the Savannah Symphony Orchestra, Hospice Savannah, and United Way.

Looking toward the future, Gulfstream plans to focus on the marketing and design of Special Requirements Aircraft (SRA), custom-made jets with special features for military use based on the corporate models. Plans are also in the works for the introduction of several other new and exciting aircraft.

It's no surprise that in 1988, one of the record-breaking Gulfstream IV models was christened "Pursuit of Perfection." Employees and customers alike understand that performance, efficiency, and quality are the foundations of success at Gulfstream Aerospace Corporation.

EM Industries, Inc.

The EM Industries, Inc. facility, located on the Savannah River in west Chatham County, has a set of dual purposes which seemingly "span the spectrum": manufacturing chemicals that control and subdue light, and producing pigments that radiate luster and sheen. These chemicals and pigments, which subdue and enhance, are sold worldwide for use in everyday products.

The Savannah plant is part of EM Industries' Chemicals and Pigments Division headquartered in Hawthorne, New York. EM is the U.S. arm of E. Merck, a pharmaceutical and chemical concern based in Darmstadt, Germany. Founded in 1668 as a small pharmacy, E. Merck today is a global organization with annual sales close to $3 billion, more than 21,000 employees, and manufacturing operations in 40 countries.

The Savannah plant produces luster pigments—all of which have metallic or pearlescent qualities—for automotive, industrial, and cosmetic uses. Pigments produced specifically for use in cosmetics are marketed under the trade names Timiron, Colorona, Dicrona, Bicrona, Nailsyn, and Naturon. Sold under the trade name Afflairs, the pigments manufactured for automotive and industrial purposes are actually non-toxic, synthetic, metal oxide-coated mica flakes. Afflairs are used in a variety of products, including automobile paints, printing inks, packaging materials, and wallcoverings.

Also at the Savannah plant are a research and development facility that serves the Chemicals and Pigments group, and technical service laboratories for automotive and industrial pigments.

In addition, the "light-controlling" chemicals manufactured in Savannah are applied to all types of lenses to subdue light and keep reflections to a minimum. Lenses in cameras, eyeglasses, and microscopes are commonly coated with these thin film-coating chemicals produced by EM under the trade name Patinals. The chemicals are carefully tested at the plant in order to meet stringent industry standards for transparency and power-handling ability.

IN SAVANNAH SINCE 1978

E. Merck established EM Industries in the United States in 1971. In a little over 20 years, the company has expanded its operations dramatically, with facilities in 10 cities employing 800 people. In addition to the Chemicals and Pigments Division, EM Industries has three

other divisions with a U.S. presence—EM Science, EM Diagnostics, and EM Pharmaceuticals—which manufacture such products as high purity reagent chemicals, hospital test kits, clinical reagents, cardiovascular drugs, and allergens for immunotherapy.

Company officials chose to open a manufacturing plant in Savannah in 1978 after carefully considering several locations throughout the South. "Savannah was attractive because of a very good infrastructure," says Heinz Reichel, vice president of operations in Savannah. The company's 200-acre tract of land on O'Leary Road is close to the port with direct connection to the Savannah River and just minutes away from State Highway 21, Interstate 95, and the Savannah International Airport.

Locally, EM Industries employs 100 men and women who are chemists, production operators, and office workers. According to Reichel, the company's Savannah work force adheres to a set of tenets honored worldwide by EM employees: service to the customer, respect for the individual, commitment to excellence, teamwork, safety, responsible care of the environment, honesty and integrity, and innovation and creativity. "We believe that our pursuit of these values will assure continued profitability and growth of EM Industries and its employees," says Reichel.

Getting involved in the community where each EM facility is located is also a priority of the company, and the Savannah operation is no exception. A United Way contributor, the Savannah plant is also an active member of the Chamber of Commerce, with representatives serving on committees devoted to education and environmental concerns. On Reichel's desk sits a Civil War-era cannonball that was presented to the company when it donated funds to restore one of the huge cannons at Old Fort Jackson on the Savannah River.

The company also encourages Savannahians to visit the plant by offering regular tours of the facility and planning frequent open houses. "We are anxious to inform area residents of our purpose here," says Reichel.

For nearly 15 years, EM Industries has been a thriving local employer and active corporate citizen. With the vast resources of a parent company that has experienced over three centuries of growth and success, EM Industries looks forward to a long and productive future in Savannah.

Top: EM's Pigment Production facility in Savannah manufactures luster pigments for automotive, industrial, and cosmetic uses. Bottom: Another facility at the Savannah plant houses the Technical Service Center and Quality Control. *(Photo: Joseph Byrd)*

Left: Heinz Reichel, vice president of operations in Savannah.

River Street was, for many years, composed of mostly dilapidated cotton warehouses and muddy trails. In 1977, Savannah spent $7 million to revitalize the area. Now, its brick promenade is one of the popular places to walk in town, and more than 75 boutiques, gift shops, restaurants, taverns, studios, and museums are located in the old warehouses. Festivals on River Street attract more than 450,000 visitors a year.

JOSEPH BYRD

1 9 9 2

1983
Patrick O. Shay & Associates

1985
ClubHouse Inn

1985
Kemira, Inc.

1985
MedStar Ambulance Services

1985
Savannah Realty

1986
Memorial Home Care

1987
Intermarine USA

1987
Price Waterhouse-Savannah

1987
Southbridge at Savannah Quarters

1990
Inglesby, Falligant, Horne, Courington & Nash, P.C.

▲ JOSEPH BYRD

Stone Container Corporation casts an industrial skyline-like reflection when photographed from the Houlihan Bridge, which crosses the Savannah River on Highway 17.

Patrick O. Shay & Associates

Choosing Savannah came naturally for Patrick Shay. After earning a Master of Architecture from Clemson University, he wanted to settle somewhere that offered both the natural beauty of the low country and the vibrant urban environment he experienced while living in Genoa, Italy. "My background and education led me to Savannah," he explains. "Living abroad gave me a great appreciation for cities that are urbane in character, yet human in scale. There's a genuinely European quality of life here."

Since founding his own practice in 1983, Shay has designed his firm to respond creatively to the individual needs of his clients. "While many firms tend toward specialization and repetitive design, we choose to create one-of-a-kind places where people live, work, and enjoy life," he says. "Computers have become an important tool in the design process, but nothing can replace the human imagination."

Creativity shows in the firm's work. Whether in the rehabilitation of a historic structure or a new construction project, a commitment to innovative solutions is apparent.

A REPUTATION FOR RESULTS

Patrick O. Shay & Associates has designed several award-winning buildings, including the Allen E. Paulson

For nearly a decade, Patrick O. Shay & Associates has offered its design expertise to diverse projects, from churches *(Photo: Gary Knight)* to the award-winning Allen E. Paulson Softball Complex *(Photo: Steven P. Mosch)*.

Softball Complex and Liberty Savings Bank's regional headquarters. "While we take pride in our awards, the bottom line is results," says Shay. "That means successfully addressing our clients' functional, scheduling, and budgetary needs, as well as aesthetics."

Successfully completed projects include an athletic center for Benedictine Military School, the Deer Creek Golf Club at the Landings, and over 80,000 square feet of office tenant improvements in the Bank South Centre. "We encourage our prospective clients to evaluate the quality of our experience against that of our competitors," explains Shay, "because we have earned our reputation with results."

PROFESSIONAL TEAM PLAYERS

One of the secrets of the firm's success has been building teams that include project managers, designers, outside consultants, and most importantly, the client. "In this way we can address the specific needs of the project without losing sight of the big picture," says Shay, "and the design team can be customized to suit the project's individual requirements."

In addition, each project gets personal attention. "I am closely involved in every project we undertake," emphasizes Shay, "while guiding our design team members to execute the design objectives." At Patrick O. Shay & Associates, teamwork means working with code officials, consultants, contractors, and clients.

DEVOTED TO SAVANNAH

Patrick Shay's commitment to community service offers insight into his leadership skills. A key member of Savannah's organizing committee which assisted in Atlanta's successful bid for the 1996 Olympic Games, Shay also serves on the Board of Directors of the Chamber of Commerce. He is the founder and president of the Savannah Maritime Festival, a celebration of the cultural and seafaring spirit of the community. As an active member of the Historic District Board of Review, Shay encourages urban development that displays respect for its historical context.

"Being actively involved with the community has helped me make connections with people who make things happen," Shay says. "These connections help us to better serve our clients in the role of advocate as well as architect."

Because of the sensitive historical, urban, and environmental conditions which are unique to Savannah, prospective developers, tenants, and residents find that they need someone to lead them through the process of obtaining required permits. "Being able to cut through the red tape is often the difference between a successful project and a nightmare," says Shay. "Because we know our business, listen carefully to our clients, and know how to guide a project through the maze, we have developed a reputation for success."

Savannah Realty

A combination of hard work and pride of ownership has helped propel Savannah Realty to the forefront of the local real estate industry. Established in 1985 by Judy Nease and Glenda Ganem, the firm specializes in residential real estate. During its relatively short history, Savannah Realty has earned a sterling reputation for serving its clients well.

Nease and Ganem are longtime Savannah businesswomen who started the company literally out of the trunks of their cars. Today, just seven years later, they operate from five spacious suites in the Park South office complex on Savannah's southside, and their company signs have become a familiar sight throughout the city.

Statistics offer further proof of the firm's rapid rise to a leadership position among local realtors. In 1991, Savannah Realty closed sales on 295 homes, or 11 percent of total real estate sales in the area. That level of success, unique in a company its size, has earned Savannah Realty the top position in its market.

BUILDING A SOLID REPUTATION

Nease and Ganem attribute the company's success to a highly structured, professional management style and a commitment to client satisfaction. "We have built a reputation for ourselves and our company," Ganem says. "That professional attitude is carried throughout the company."

Ganem's 20 years in the Savannah real estate market and Nease's 13 years of office management experience ensure a high level of expertise and performance. The two train every member of the Savannah Realty team—including more than 20 associates, five support personnel, and a relocation director—in the best techniques of the industry. "A great strength of Savannah Realty is our staff's high degree of dedication to the profession," says Nease. "In fact, more than half of our associates are members of the Savannah Board of Realtors Million Dollar Club."

As a member of the Multiple Listing Service, Savannah Realty and its clients benefit from cooperation among local brokers. This affiliation, which helps simplify the often hectic process of buying or selling a home, allows the sales staff greater access to homes and properties throughout Savannah and surrounding counties.

"We feel that a large part of our success stems from a true desire to help our customers," Nease says. "We are very professional in our relations with them; we're not a loosely run operation. Our associates view their jobs as full-time careers, not sideline ventures. And they have certain guidelines and policies they must follow."

Ganem adds, "When we set up the business, we established specific job descriptions for ourselves. Even today, we stick to those original guidelines because it is in the best interest of the company and its success."

Although the sales team at Savannah Realty has included men in the past, the staff today is primarily women. According to Ganem and Nease, they didn't actually plan it that way. Through the years they have discovered that women often make the final decision when a family is buying a home. "The woman usually has very definite ideas about what she wants," Ganem explains, "and she is often able to communicate those ideas more clearly to another woman. Perhaps that's why there are so many women real estate agents."

SUCCESS THROUGH PERSONAL COMMITMENT

Despite a sluggish economy over the past several years, Savannah Realty has survived and thrived by relying on a simple, "back-to-basics" philosophy. "We have weathered the recession just fine," Nease says. "At one point we did cut back on housekeeping. We had the cleaning company service our building one day a week instead of two, and we took turns taking out the trash ourselves!"

Such strategy is typical at Savannah Realty and of the women who have seen their firm flourish throughout its first years in business. That unmistakable pride of ownership, clearly reflected by Ganem and Nease, is the key to their day-in, day-out dedication to the business.

"A great strength of Savannah Realty is our staff's high degree of dedication to the profession," says Judy Nease, co-owner. "In fact, more than half of our associates are members of the Savannah Board of Realtors Million Dollar Club."

Established in 1985 by Glenda Ganem (left) and Judy Nease, Savannah Realty specializes in residential real estate.

Kemira, Inc.

As Savannah's third-largest industrial employer, providing jobs for nearly 800 local men and women, Kemira, Inc. is one of the city's most vital industries. The plant, located on a 1,640-acre tract on the Savannah River, has been an important part of the community since 1985. Kemira is one of only five companies in the United States producing titanium dioxide, a highly demanded white pigment most commonly used in paints.

In its natural state, titanium ore is a fine black grain found in concentrations of sand. Though the ore can be seen on virtually any beach, it occurs in large concentrations in certain areas of Africa and Australia. At Kemira, this black material is chemically transformed into pure, white titanium dioxide, a stable, non-toxic pigment valued for its many and varied uses.

The product is marketed primarily to the paint and coatings industry as a replacement for highly toxic lead-based pigment; in fact, about half of the titanium dioxide produced at Kemira annually is sold for this purpose. The paper industry represents the second-largest market for the substance. Because titanium dioxide is a safe pigment that gives products such desirable qualities as brightness, opacity, and durability, its potential uses extend to other areas as well, including fibers, plastics, printing inks, cosmetics, and even food additives.

A SUBSIDIARY OF KEMIRA OY

Kemira, Inc. in Savannah is the sole U.S. subsidiary of Kemira Oy, an international chemical corporation headquartered in Helsinki, Finland. In 1919, the company opened its first plant in Finland to produce fertilizer to help enhance food production after World War I. Kemira Oy grew over the years, building new production facilities throughout Finland and earning a reputation as a well-known and trusted chemical conglomerate with bases throughout Europe. Kemira began further expansion in the 1980s, including the acquisition of the Savannah plant in 1985. Today, Kemira Oy has a presence in approximately 20 countries on several continents. Its products include fertilizers, agricultural and industrial chemicals, paints, and titanium dioxide, among others.

Although the Savannah plant's manufacturing capability is concentrated on titanium dioxide, Kemira also markets byproducts and intermediates created during its production process. Gypsum, Kemira's largest byproduct, is commonly used in wallboard. It is also marketed as a soil conditioner and shell hardener for Georgia peanuts. Likewise, carbon dioxide generated during Kemira's waste treatment process is sold to soft drink companies to carbonate beverages.

Titanium dioxide (TiO2), used primarily in paints, offers a safe alternative to lead-based pigment. Far right: TiO2 gives brightness, opacity, and durability to a variety of products.

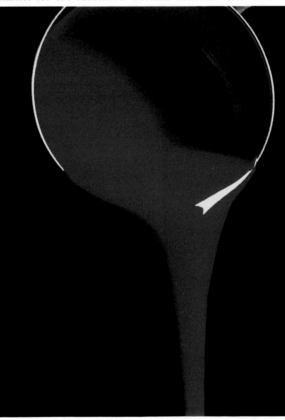

As a concerned and environmentally responsible industrial citizen, Kemira, Inc. is proud of its comprehensive programs to utilize byproducts and intermediates and to neutralize all process waste. Given its location on the Savannah River, the company takes special care to meet and surpass EPA guidelines to protect the environment and the citizens of Savannah—a level of commitment that has not gone unrecognized.

In 1988, Kemira received a special Air Quality Award from the Georgia Department of Natural Resources and the Business Council of Georgia. In order to further reduce hazardous waste, the company instituted significant operational and procedural changes in 1989. These efforts were rewarded two years later when Kemira was recognized as the 1991 Land Quality Environmental Citizen of the Year by the Business Council of Georgia. Officials at Kemira cite environmental responsibility and safety as a top priority and pledge that, as the company expands, it will continue to function within EPA guidelines.

A Good Corporate Citizen

Since its move to Savannah in 1985, the company has worked to be a good corporate citizen and neighbor. Kemira employees are active members of the Chamber of Commerce, Rotary Club, and other groups. They also pledge their time and money to the Red Cross and the United Way.

Seven days a week, 24 hours a day, Kemira employees play their individual roles in the production of titanium dioxide. With an annual payroll exceeding $33 million locally and an economic impact of a half-billion dollars, the company has established itself as one of the area's most vital industries. Through its programs for community involvement and environmentalism, Kemira, Inc. has proven itself a good neighbor with a bright future in Savannah.

Above: The Kemira Agro plant is located in Uusikaupunki, Finland. Left: Kemira, Inc. occupies a 1,640-acre tract on the Savannah River.

ClubHouse Inn

Today's business and vacation travelers have a variety of economical accommodations to choose from along America's interstates and highways. But oftentimes lodging that is pleasing to the pocketbook is deflating to the traveler's spirit. Most offer no frills—just an ordinary room with a couple of beds, a television, and a clean bathroom. And for breakfast, guests must rely on the in-house coffee shop for a humdrum meal or settle for nearby fast food restaurants.

The hotel's club-like amenities and home-like ambience offer a fresh alternative for business travelers. Above right: Nationwide, 15 ClubHouse Inns deliver the comfort and extra amenities that every traveler deserves.

The exception to the rule of affordable lodging in Savannah is ClubHouse Inn, which offers travelers no-cost extras that even deluxe hotels often charge for: a free hot breakfast buffet, complimentary two-hour evening cocktail reception, free local phone calls, remote control cable television with free movies, swimming pool, and an indoor whirlpool spa. The hotel, which features club-like amenities with a home-like ambience, is located at 6800 Abercorn Street, making it accessible to interstate highways and the business district.

In addition, the stylishly decorated, oversized guest rooms at ClubHouse Inn feature a king-size bed or two double beds, desks with ample work space, large bathrooms with separate vanities, and closets with full-length mirrors. Of the 138 rooms at the Savannah ClubHouse Inn, 16 are two-room suites with separate living and sleeping quarters, as well as a dining area with wet bar, microwave oven, refrigerator, and coffee maker. In addition, the hotel's two meeting rooms can accommodate from five to 50 people.

Savannah's ClubHouse Inn, which opened in June 1989, is one of 15 similar hotels managed by Club-House/Innco of Overland Park, Kansas. ClubHouse Inns are also located in Albuquerque, New Mexico; Chicago, Illinois; Kansas City, Missouri; Topeka, Wichita, and Overland Park, Kansas; Knoxville and Nashville, Tennessee; Lansing, Michigan; Omaha, Nebraska; Pittsburgh, Pennsylvania; and Atlanta and Valdosta, Georgia. Plans are in the works for more than a dozen new ClubHouse Inns as well.

A SUCCESSFUL CONCEPT

The idea of a limited service, mid-sized hotel catering primarily to the business traveler was born in the early 1980s when Innco Hospitality, which has been in the lodging business since 1976, sensed a shift in the industry to a more cost-conscious consumer attitude. By 1985, the first ClubHouse Inn opened in Wichita, Kansas. All properties today feature oversized rooms and an amenities package that gives guests extra value for their dollar. ClubHouse Inns differ from other full-service hotels in that they do not have restaurants and large ballrooms, common features that can be a significant drain on a hotel's profitability.

According to Chairman David Aull of ClubHouse/ Innco, the moderate price for a ClubHouse Inn room or suite has proved to be a winner with business travelers and vacationers alike. "We're popular with everybody looking for the right accommodations at the right price," says Aull. Business travelers have even voted their approval for ClubHouse Inn: In 1990, 1991, and 1992, *Business Travel News*, a bi-monthly publication of the travel industry, published surveys in which travelers consistently rated ClubHouse Inn number one among mid-sized hotels in service and at the top in price/value categories.

"We have a very good following at our five hotels in the Southeast," Aull says. "Savannah presented a nice opportunity for us because of the government offices and businesses that involve traveling executives. Since its opening, the hotel has also developed a following with leisure travelers visiting the area."

According to Aull, ClubHouse Inn is not just a nice alternative to the bare-bones economy hotel, or a low-budget substitute for the multi-story luxury hotel. Its success in Savannah proves that price-conscious guests can enjoy the comfort and extra amenities that every traveler deserves.

Tuesday, 10:05 p.m. A MedStar ambulance responds to an auto accident scene in downtown Savannah. The dispatcher carefully monitors the situation: Three victims of the crash... Extrication in progress... A young woman with possible head injuries is being transported to the hospital. Minutes later, another call comes in: Possible heart attack... CPR (cardiopulmonary resuscitation) in progress... A MedStar team arrives and works fervently to restore the patient's pulse... He will make it... After arrival at the hospital, a paramedic checks on the accident victim... She is stable. The next hour holds different challenges.

Each year, the dedicated employees of MedStar Ambulance Services handle thousands of similar calls, saving lives throughout the Chatham County area. Affiliated with Memorial Medical Center, MedStar is the largest ambulance service in southeast Georgia. It employs more than 90 people, including paramedics, EMTs (emergency medical technicians), EMDs (emergency medical dispatchers), and fleet operations and training personnel.

MedStar answered nearly half of Chatham County's 21,000 emergency calls in 1991. The company also provides paramedics and dispatchers for LifeStar, Memorial's emergency helicopter service.

Emergency responses account for only about half of MedStar's annual business, according to Director Stephen Mobley, a 34-year veteran of the ambulance and emergency care business. "Our other transport services include neonatal transports, hospital-to-hospital transfers, and transporting dialysis and nursing home patients to and from the hospital or to physician offices," he says.

MedStar's operations center is located at Memorial Medical Center, where emergency calls are received directly or from 911 operators at the Chatham County Police Department. When a MedStar EMD receives a call, the caller's location is entered into a computerized communications system known as MEDICS®, the only tracking system of its kind currently being used by an ambulance service in Chatham County. With cross-street reference and map-grid features, MEDICS® will indicate to the dispatcher the nearest cross-street of any given address, enabling the closest available MedStar ambulance to respond.

With ambulances stationed at seven locations throughout the city, MedStar's 20-vehicle fleet includes ambulances, a critical care unit, a supervisor's vehicle, and Angel 3—a neonatal unit that serves 24 counties in southeast Georgia. Each vehicle is equipped with state-of-the-art medical equipment, such as EKG monitors and defibrillators for heart patients. The critical care unit is also equipped with ventilators, IV pumps, and other more advanced prehospital equipment that is not usually carried on an ambulance.

MedStar Ambulance Services

HIGHLY TRAINED STAFF

The paramedics and EMTs who staff the emergency vehicles are experienced professionals. In addition to state certification as EMTs and paramedics, these professionals receive rigorous training through MedStar's training and development department. MedStar was the first ambulance service in Georgia to implement the FailSafe Driving System®, a traffic and vehicle management program for professional drivers that reduces risk and costs, and produces a safer ride for both patients and crews. MedStar drivers also are required to receive National Safety Council certification prior to being allowed to drive.

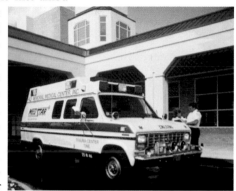

Mobley, who was selected as the 1991-92 Director of the Year by the Emergency Medical Service Directors Association of Georgia, was instrumental in establishing MedStar in 1985 and has served as its director since that time. Today, Mobley is actively involved with the Georgia EMS Council, for which he serves as secretary. He also serves as chairman of the Region IX Emergency Medical Service Council, which covers 24 counties in southeast Georgia.

Mobley believes MedStar's purpose is two-fold: to provide the best possible emergency medical service to Chatham County residents and to be an active participant in community activities. As part of its community service, MedStar provides standby ambulance coverage for most major events in Chatham County. MedStar also is the primary emergency medical service that participates in local disaster drills and simulations. Its paramedics and EMTs teach cardiopulmonary resuscitation and basic first aid to high school students, while "Andy," the MedStar robot ambulance, visits elementary schools to teach younger children about safety issues and when to call 911.

In all its roles—as lifesaver, transport service, community servant, and teacher—MedStar Ambulance Services sets the highest standards of professionalism. Above all, MedStar's team of experienced personnel is dedicated to responding to emergencies and saving lives in Savannah.

Top: With ambulances stationed at seven locations throughout the city, MedStar's 20-vehicle fleet provides an indispensable service to the community. Bottom: MedStar's operations center, located at Memorial Medical Center, utilizes a state-of-the-art computerized dispatch system.

Memorial Home Care

In recent years Memorial Medical Center, the fastest growing medical facility in southeast Georgia, has become a leading provider of home health care services. Under the auspices of Memorial Home Care, the medical center supplies home care services and products such as medical equipment and supplies, health care staff representing numerous specialties, and infusion therapy programs to patients who prefer or require treatment in the home.

Recognizing that home care is an essential and growing aspect of the health care field, Memorial Medical Center acquired AmeriCare Home Health Services and AmeriCare Nursing Services in 1986, and Paragon HomeCare and Paragon Nursing in 1991. Memorial's involvement with home infusion was launched in 1987 with the opening of Southern Home Therapeutics.

"The growth of Memorial in the home care services field reflects the hospital's commitment to continued progress," says Ellen Repella, Memorial's executive director of home care. "We are dedicated to delivering health care services with a caring attitude and the highest professionalism, whether in a home or a hospital setting."

Approximately 3,000 part-time, full-time, and casual workers are employed by the AmeriCare and Paragon agencies in Georgia, Florida, and Texas. Home care services are available 24 hours a day, seven days a week to patients of all ages, the majority of whom are at least 65 years old.

The AmeriCare companies have four home health agencies in Savannah, Tifton, Vidalia, and Waycross, Georgia, with 33 branch offices located throughout south Georgia. In Florida, Paragon HomeCare operates four agencies in Clearwater, Daytona, Sanford, and Bushnell, as well as 22 branches scattered throughout the state. Paragon Nursing is located in Clearwater, Daytona, Orlando, and New Port Richey. Paragon also operates agencies in Austin and San Antonio, Texas, with six branches in other parts of the state. Plans are under way to open 22 new locations of AmeriCare and Paragon in the coming years.

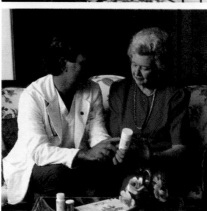

Top: An AmeriCare physical therapist assists a patient with walking. Bottom: An AmeriCare nurse offers instructions on medication.

COMPREHENSIVE HOME CARE SERVICES

AmeriCare Home Health Services and Paragon Home-Care are Medicare/Medicaid-certified home health agencies that provide nursing care, social support, and rehabilitative services to patients in their places of residence. Registered and licensed practical nurses, home health aides, social workers, and physical, speech, and occupational therapists perform the various services that, Repella emphasizes, are administered under the supervision of the patient's physician. "We don't take the place of the doctor," she says. "We carry out the physician's plan of care."

Carrying out the doctor's treatment plan may involve dispensing oxygen supplements, supervising sleep monitoring, administering intravenous therapies, teaching members of the patient's family to change dressings or give injections, and assisting patients with personal hygiene, among many other services.

AmeriCare Nursing Services and Paragon Nursing are private duty home care agencies that have nurses, therapists, homemakers, and live-in workers on staff. The nursing staff includes registered nurses, licensed practical nurses, and certified nurses aides with specialties in pediatrics, post-partum, kidney dialysis, respiratory, rehabilitation, cancer, intravenous therapy, antibiotic care, and psychiatric, neurological, and cardiac care. AmeriCare homemakers are non-health care workers who help patients with housekeeping responsibilities such as meal preparation and laundry, while live-in workers provide an around-the-clock presence in the home and assist in household duties.

Other divisions of Memorial Home Care also play important roles in at-home patient care. Southern Home Therapeutics works in conjunction with other home care services to provide a safe and cost-effective alternative to prolonged hospitalization for patients needing short- and long-term infusion (intravenous) services. The home infusion nurse can make home visits, provide guidance, answer questions, monitor the patient's progress, and supervise and maintain proper care of the patient's catheter.

AmeriCare Medical Equipment, also under the Memorial Home Care umbrella, offers at-home patients easy access to quality medical equipment. The company is a supplier of durable medical products such as ventilators, portable oxygen equipment, sleep monitors, beds and bedding accessories, bath and toilet aids, and wheelchairs.

In Savannah and all of its markets, Memorial Home Care strives to supply a comprehensive range of health care services and products. Most importantly, each Memorial agency is committed to delivering the finest in at-home services with unsurpassed professionalism and a caring attitude.

Southbridge at Savannah Quarters

The convenient location, tranquil setting, and small-town flavor of Southbridge at Savannah Quarters is Southern hospitality at its very best. With an award-winning golf course, first-class tennis facilities, and one of the few equestrian centers in the area, Southbridge is a residential community with plenty to offer people of all ages—from young families to retirees.

It's an inviting scene to imagine: Sunlight peeks through a thick canopy of trees onto a wooded lane; a family on bicycles pedals past homes with well-kept lawns; an opening in the landscape reveals a golf cart on a manicured green; around the bend are the swimming pool and tennis courts; and less than eight miles away is Savannah's unique historic district.

At Southbridge, this vista is not just an ideal in a developer's mind. It's plain and simple everyday life with a touch of class. And Hall Development, Inc., the company responsible for bringing it all to life in Savannah, would have it no other way.

A WELL-PLANNED COMMUNITY

Southbridge is the first phase of the 5,800-acre Savannah Quarters, a development at the intersection of Interstates 95 and 16 that eventually will include 10,000 homes, 958 acres of shopping, retail, and commercial space, six championship golf courses, office parks, and a destination point entertainment complex.

Southbridge began taking shape in 1987, when Hall Development of Myrtle Beach, South Carolina presented its plans to the Savannah community. A well-established firm with three decades of experience, Hall has completed similar projects in Durham, North Carolina and Columbia, South Carolina. Additionally, four first-class projects are in the works in Myrtle Beach.

Southbridge includes 1,100 acres of gently rolling woodlands, dense with century-old trees dripping with Spanish moss. The center of the community is the Southbridge Golf Club, co-host of the Georgia Open and the site for numerous charity tournaments. The attractive clubhouse is often teeming with activity, whether in the pro shop or in the grill. Outside, the club has a large teaching facility and a secluded practice range. The course itself is a challenging 18-hole masterpiece designed by noted golf course architect Rees Jones.

Facilities at the Southbridge Swim & Racquet Club include a competition-size pool, a spa, 12 clay tennis courts, and two hard courts. Also on the grounds is the Sa-Hi Riding Academy with complete boarding and instructional facilities, as well as miles of bridle trails.

All of this is just minutes from downtown Savannah, a selling point which clearly bolsters the appeal of the community. According to a survey conducted by Hall Development, convenience is key at Southbridge. In fact, location, followed by neighborhood setting, were the top two reasons residents gave when asked why they selected Southbridge.

A DIVERSE MIX OF RESIDENTS

A diverse mix of residents live in the homes already constructed amid the tall pines at Southbridge. Neighbors wave to one another on the golf course, at the tennis center, by the pool, or during a leisurely stroll down the street. They also keep up with each other through a monthly newsletter published by Hall Development.

All Southbridge homes border the golf course, scenic lagoons, or peaceful wooded areas. They also show a tremendous amount of architectural variety, from classic Williamsburg to traditional cottage. Though architectural covenants are required at Southbridge, restrictions are in place to uphold quality, not to be cumbersome. At Southbridge, everything doesn't look alike, and it's not an exclusive community catering only to the wealthy. The surprising affordability of Southbridge homes may well be the most important family value the development can offer a homeowner.

Mark Hall, Southbridge project director, has a tremendous amount of confidence in the project and in Savannah. He and his family live at Southbridge and are active in civic affairs. "This town is going places, and we plan to do everything we can to help it along," he says. "We are responsible citizens because we have a commitment to this community. Savannah is a great place to live and do business."

Left: Homes at Southbridge vary in architectural style, from classic Williamsburg to traditional cottage. Below: Residents enjoy the award-winning 18-hole golf course at Southbridge.

Intermarine USA

A revolution in large marine composite structure design and development is taking place on the banks of the Savannah River. Intermarine USA, an Italian shipbuilding company, is making maritime history through the successful application of modern marine technology in the construction of Osprey-class mine hunters for the U.S. Navy.

Today, Intermarine USA (top) occupies the site where the Savannah Machine and Foundry Company (bottom) thrived during World War II. Above right: Inside the mold, layer after layer of GRP is hand-laid to form what will ultimately become MHC 52 Heron.

SHIPBUILDING IN SAVANNAH

Savannah, as well as the rest of the country, endured dark and foreboding times during World War II. With local men on military duty throughout the world, the Savannah economy was decidedly sluggish. But amid the economic hardship, about 1,500 men and women worked at breakneck speed at the Savannah Machine and Foundry Company on the riverfront to build minesweepers, ships that sweep and clear enemy explosives. When the war ended, Army-Navy E-Award flags fluttered proudly in the breeze at the shipyard, symbolizing the entire community's role in the country's defense. Today, the E-plaque is on display at historic Fort Jackson.

Shipbuilding declined in Savannah following World War II, and the old shipyard functioned as a ship repair facility under several different owners over the next few decades. But since the late 1980s, exciting things have been happening at the riverfront site where so many Savannahians proudly worked during the war: shipbuilding has returned to Savannah.

ITALY COMES TO TOWN

Intermarine USA was not even a gleam in Savannah's eye when in the mid-1980s the U.S. Navy initiated a program for the design and construction of a new class of ships, specifically designed for mine hunting, that would be more sophisticated and technologically advanced than earlier minesweepers. In 1987, the Navy selected the

Italian company Intermarine SpA to design and build a mine hunter for the difficult task of hunting in harbors, channels, and coastal waters where moored and bottom mines could be detected and neutralized.

Since 1979, Intermarine SpA has built mine hunters of Glass Reinforced Plastic (GRP) for the Italian Navy, the Royal Malaysian Navy, and the Nigerian Navy. The company is part of the Chemicals division of the Feruzzi Group, an Italian industrial concern also involved in grain trading, agriculture, and research. With more than 300 plants, in 30 countries, on three continents, Feruzzi employs over 114,000 people worldwide.

Several factors attracted Intermarine to Savannah: the existing shipyard, the deep navigable waterway with access to the ocean, and the city's proximity to the Navy's Mine Warfare Headquarters in Charleston, South Carolina.

Once Savannah was established as the home of Intermarine USA, the company began overhauling and updating the old shipyard. Today, the site includes a dry dock, a wet slip basin, a 380-foot riverfront dock, and a state-of-the-art rail-launch system. Intermarine also completed $2 million in pier improvements and refurbished a 50-ton crane to serve both the wet and dry docks. Millions more dollars were spent refurbishing the riverfront facility, which sits on 23.5 acres owned by the company. The 225,650-square-foot complex now includes a 71,168-square-foot GRP shop, a piping and mechanical department, an electric/electronic shop, a warehouse, offices, and a modern chemical and physical properties test laboratory for composite materials. Intermarine USA also has a marine engineering and design department that, along with logistics personnel, provides complete engineering services to the marine and composites industries.

BUILDING OSPREY-CLASS MINE HUNTERS

Production of the first Osprey-class mine hunter began in May 1988. Major components of the ship, such as the hull, decks, and superstructure, are built by laminating layer after layer of fiberglass inside giant molds, giving the vessel tremendous strength. All raw materials used in the ship's construction are tested in extensive shock and explosion trials. "These ships are meticulously designed to withstand high levels of shock resulting from near underwater explosions," says Ted Young, managing director for the company. "We run a sophisticated but lean and efficient shipbuilding operation."

In March 1991, Intermarine USA launched its first U.S. Navy ship into the Savannah River at the former site of Savannah Machine and Foundry Company. The vessel was the first in a series of Osprey-class mine hunters that Intermarine is under contract to build for the U.S. Navy. Many of the company's 700 highly skilled employees were on hand for the colorful ceremony as Colleen Nunn, wife of U.S. Senator Sam Nunn, christened the ship.

"The Osprey mine hunter is a sophisticated vessel equipped with the latest in high-tech gear," says Young. "At 880 tons and 188 feet in length, it is the largest displacement fiberglass ship in the world."

According to Young, a mine hunter differs from a sweeper in that it is equipped to detect and destroy mines. The ships are constructed completely from GRP and take about four years to build and test. Intermarine's second ship was launched into the Savannah River in March 1992.

A QUALITY EMPLOYER

As the city's fourth largest employer, Intermarine USA is a company that civic leaders and the business community are proud to have in Savannah. In fact, visiting dignitaries and political officials often tour the company's impressive facilities. According to Young, it's also a great place to work.

"Intermarine USA adheres to TQM—Total Quality Management," he explains. "Employees stand behind every piece of equipment or component they are making. They want people to know they do a good job and are proud of what they accomplish. The end result is quality workmanship which, along with other obvious benefits, saves lives and taxpayers' money."

Intermarine is a leader in the Savannah Area Chamber of Commerce's program for a "Drug Free Workplace." As a "Pace Setter" organization, the company plays an active role in the community to support the program's zero tolerance, drug-free efforts.

Intermarine is also a participating member of the Savannah Business Group, a consortium of several major Savannah industries, which has contracted for group health insurance at reduced rates. These and other efforts go a long way to help the company control health care costs for its employees and their 2,100 family members.

Important to employees and Savannah residents alike is the fact that Intermarine USA is an environmentally safe and clean company. "We have an environmental conscience," says Young, "We don't put anything harmful into the air, the water, or the ground."

Likewise, the company is proud of its employee involvement in a variety of community activities. Intermarine workers participate in the educational partnership program of the Savannah Area Chamber of Commerce that pairs businesses and schools. They also coach soccer teams, lead Scout troops, and bowl with company-sponsored leagues, among other activities.

"Intermarine USA equals pride," says Young. "We are extremely proud of our employees. They *are* Intermarine. We are also proud of Savannah and Chatham County. Our pride in our nation and the Navy carries over in our product. Everything we do reflects the pride and confidence our people have in America. Intermarine is proof positive that a company can be a strong defense contractor and a good corporate citizen."

Above: Prior to sea trials, Intermarine employees install and test all machinery and equipment. Left: Senator Sam Nunn helped celebrate the launching of the first Osprey-class mine hunter in March 1991.

Price Waterhouse-Savannah

Price Waterhouse-Savannah takes pride in the many benefits the firm offers its clients: Each client is assured quality accounting services from one of the premier accounting firms in the world; the firm has a distinguished service record dating from the organization's founding over 130 years ago; and it offers numerous services through a comprehensive management and consulting network. Locally, this distinguished heritage was strengthened by Price Waterhouse's 1987 merger with a highly respected accounting firm founded in Savannah.

Price Waterhouse has maintained a presence in Savannah since the early 1970s when the firm's Atlanta office began serving several local clients. In the mid-1970s, the firm continued its relationships with local clients through an affiliation with Spillane, Rhoads, Lebey, Cann and Sieg, the largest and oldest accounting firm in Savannah. In 1987, Price Waterhouse merged with Spillane, Rhoads, Lebey and Sieg and moved into offices downtown in the First Union National Bank Building overlooking Johnson Square.

The largest accounting firm in Savannah, Price Waterhouse employs 50 men and women who work as partners, managers, senior and staff accountants, and support personnel.

"Price Waterhouse considers it an honor to have merged with such a trusted accounting firm," says Donald Bambarger, managing partner in the Savannah office. "With our national and international relationships, we believe we are offering Savannahians the best of both worlds—full service with a local touch."

A LOCAL FIRM WITH GLOBAL RESOURCES

Founded in England in 1859, Price Waterhouse is a worldwide professional organization of accountants, auditors, tax advisers, and management consultants. Considered one of the top accounting firms in the world, Price Waterhouse has 458 offices (including 115 in the United States) in 110 countries. In fact, Price Waterhouse serves more clients listed in *Fortune* magazine's survey of America's "most admired corporations" than any other accounting firm in the United States.

Right: Professionals at Price Waterhouse-Savannah provide accounting, auditing, and tax services for a diverse roster of clients.

Underlying that distinguished reputation is a solid foundation of professionalism. The firm's professional staff are accounting majors recruited from college campuses nationwide. Price Waterhouse is recognized for employing the finest accounting talent available. Further proof of its professionalism is the fact that Price Waterhouse was the first major accounting firm to achieve a perfect score in a peer review of compliance with professional standards conducted by the American Institute of Certified Public Accountants.

The largest accounting firm in Savannah, Price Waterhouse employs 50 men and women who work as partners, managers, senior and staff accountants, and support personnel. The local office provides accounting, auditing, and tax services to its large corporate, small business, and individual clients in the food processing, manufacturing, shipping, health care, wholesale distribution, and financial industries. In addition to these local services, the firm has access to a large and comprehensive management and consulting network through its regional office in Atlanta.

"Having access to such a network is one of the major benefits of doing business with Price Waterhouse," says Bambarger. "If a client needs assistance with strategic planning, for example, we can identify the experts and put them in touch with the client. We can provide information on employee benefits, information systems, and mergers and acquisitions. Price Waterhouse offers a variety of services that aren't available in locally based accounting firms."

Price Waterhouse also maintains a full-service tax department, whose staff provides estate planning, tax consulting, and executive tax planning services. "We're able to call on our specialists in Washington and other locations to answer questions, whenever necessary, concerning the ever-changing tax laws or any tax problem," says Bambarger.

With the finest in accounting talent and resources, a local history of excellence, and more than a century of experience on a global level, Price Waterhouse-Savannah is firmly committed to continuing in its role as the city's preeminent accounting firm.

Inglesby, Falligant, Horne, Courington & Nash, P.C.

The attorneys of Inglesby, Falligant, Horne, Courington & Nash, P.C. are committed to the practice of law in the most professional manner. "Within the framework of professionalism, we are united in a common goal of doing the best possible job to serve our clients in the most cost-efficient manner," explains Sam Inglesby, president and senior member of the firm. "Depth of experience and personalized attention are what set us apart from other law firms."

While the firm was established only a few years ago, most of the seven attorneys are longtime co-workers who previously practiced together at another Savannah law firm. The firm has a very active real estate practice which not only closes acquisitions and loans relating to real property located in Chatham County and neighboring counties but also works closely with zoning and other regulatory agencies.

The firm also has a strong litigation practice. "Our attorneys can promise our clients a blend of solid preparation, persuasion, advocacy, and good judgment," says Tom Nash, a partner active in litigation.

Other attorneys in the firm specialize in corporate and commercial law and the laws relating to loan transactions and bankruptcy. The business practice includes the organization of corporations, partnerships, and joint ventures, as well as the negotiation and structuring of sales, purchases, contracts, leases, and financing arrangements. The bankruptcy practitioners principally represent secured and unsecured creditors with claims in bankruptcy. Two of the attorneys routinely work on will and probate matters, including estate planning for tax savings. The firm's clients include major corporations, banks, utilities, insurance companies, and other businesses, as well as individuals.

THE ATTORNEYS

Sam Inglesby has 25 years of experience representing banks and financial institutions and practices before state and federal courts. In 1991, he was elected president of the Savannah Bar Association. A graduate of the University of Georgia Law School, he is also a member of the Georgia Defense Lawyers Association.

J. Daniel Falligant is a well known expert in the fields of commercial and residential real estate. He has served as a seminar lecturer on a number of topics for the Georgia Institute of Continuing Legal Education. A 1968 graduate of Mercer University Law School in Macon, Georgia, Falligant is a member of the Board of Governors of the State Bar of Georgia.

Kathleen Horne specializes in bankruptcy and creditors' rights. She received her law degree cum laude from the University of Georgia in 1976. Horne, who is active in the American Bankruptcy Institute and the National Conference of Bankruptcy Judges, is a frequent lecturer at bankruptcy and lending seminars.

In addition to handling the firm's business affairs, Dorothy Courington practices commercial and corporate law and, along with Dolly Chisholm, works regularly in trust and estate matters. A 1977 cum laude graduate of the University of Georgia Law School, Courington served as research editor of the *Georgia Law Review* while in school.

A magna cum laude graduate of the University of Georgia Law School in 1976, Thomas A. Nash Jr. specializes in commercial and personal litigation. He is a member of the Georgia Trial Lawyers Association and the Association of Trial Lawyers of America. He also holds a Chartered Property & Casualty Underwriters designation, which gives him great insight into insurance issues.

Dolly Chisholm and Ed Stabell are the newest attorneys in the firm. Chisholm, a 1987 graduate of Tulane University Law School, works primarily in the areas of bankruptcy and estate planning. A 1992 graduate of Mercer University Law School, Stabell works as needed with all the other attorneys while developing a field of expertise that he will follow in later years.

Beyond the office and the courtrooms, the firm's attorneys contribute countless hours to civic and charitable organizations and directly represent indigent individuals as volunteers in Georgia Legal Services programs.

IMPROVING THE QUALITY OF LIFE IN SAVANNAH

Beyond the office and the courtrooms, the firm's attorneys are actively improving the quality of life in their hometown of Savannah. They contribute countless hours to civic and charitable organizations and directly represent indigent individuals as volunteers in Georgia Legal Services programs. They have also served behind the scenes in many political campaigns.

"We are on a solid footing for the future," says Sam Inglesby. "Savannah is a great place to live and practice law. It is a growing and changing area, and we are committed to offering the best professional legal services through the '90s and into the 21st century."

Photographers

JOSEPH BYRD, photo editor for *Savannah: Crown of the Colonial Coast*, is an award-winning professional photographer in Savannah, Georgia.

Specializing in commercial photography, from product catalogs to editorial photographic illustrations, Byrd serves clients from regional hospitals to industrial corporations and coastal resorts. He is the recipient of top awards from the Florida Printing Industries, the Georgia Magazine Association and the Advertising Club of Savannah. His work has appeared in national advertising campaigns, numerous trade journals and in city, regional, and national publications.

Byrd, who was born in Tokyo, moved to Savannah at age five. He has made the city a base for his business, Joseph Byrd and Associates, and his permanent home.

GEORGE BARTHELMESS established his studio, Windsong Photography, in 1983. His areas of emphasis range from portraits and weddings to corporate and commercial projects, and his work has appeared in numerous magazines and publications. He resides in Savannah with his wife and child.

STEVE BISSON, who received a B.A. in journalism from the University of Georgia in 1976, has been the chief photographer for the *Savannah News-Press* for the past 14 years. A native of Savannah, Bisson has received numerous Associated Press and Georgia Press Association awards for his accomplishments in photojournalism.

PETER J. CAMPBELL is currently the studio manager and an associate photographer for Riley and Riley Photography in Asheville, North Carolina. His areas of emphasis include nature, corporate, and advertising photography. Campbell received a B.F.A. in photography from Savannah College of Art and Design in 1989.

JOHN CARRINGTON has worked as a staff photographer for the *Savannah News-Press* for four years. Carrington received a second-place award in black-and-white feature photography from the Georgia Press Association in 1992. Originally from Maryville, Tennessee, Carrington received a B.F.A. from Savannah College of Art and Design. His work has been published in the *Atlanta Constitution*, the *Chicago Tribune*, and *Time*.

LINDA ERZINGER, who received a B.F.A. in illustration from Savannah College of Art and Design in 1989, has been a free-lance photographer in the Savannah area for three years. Erzinger enjoys traveling as a hobby as well as a means of increasing her stock of outdoor photos. She also executes murals and illustrations.

R.T. FULLER has spent the past 27 years exploring various fields of photography, from yearbook, studio, and newspaper projects to landscape, underwater, and aerial work. Fuller currently specializes in portraiture and commercial photography. His work has been published by the Associated Press, United Press International, and the Georgia Historical Society.

PAULA GOMEZ, originally from Boulder, Colorado, joined the *Savannah News-Press* as a staff photographer in 1988. Beyond her primary commitment to news, studio, and nature photography, Gomez has also worked for the Department of Family and Children's Services on a special campaign to prevent child abuse. Gomez received her B.F.A. and M.F.A. in photography from Savannah College of Art and Design.

HERLENE R. HOPKINS, a Savannah native, manages her own "Machine and Hand Knitts" company and produces fashion photography. A graduate of Armstrong State College in Savannah, Hopkins is a retired tax examiner for the Internal Revenue Service.

LEONARD JONES II, a free-lance photographer for the past seven years, specializes in portrait, wedding, and special events photography. He serves as an audio visual director and yearbook photographer at his alma mater, Savannah State College, and as director of television ministry at his church.

DARIA LUCREE has been an associate photographer and darkroom technician for Jim Daly Photography in Savannah for three years. Currently Lucree specializes in wedding, portrait, and special events photography. A native of Clearwater, Florida, Lucree will graduate in June 1993 from Armstrong State College in Savannah.

JEFFREY M. MCSWEENEY, a staff photographer for the *Savannah News-Press* for two-and-a-half years, established a photography studio, ImageMasters, in 1992. Originally from Washington, Illinois, McSweeney earned a B.A. in communications from Eureka College in Eureka, Illinois, and an M.F.A. in photography from the Savannah College of Art and Design.

BOB MORRIS, originally from Louisville, Kentucky, has worked as a staff photographer for the *Savannah News-Press* for the past 17 years. Throughout his career, Morris has received numerous Associated Press and Georgia Press Association awards for his contributions to photojournalism.

CHARLES RIBBENS, a graduate of Savannah College of Art and Design, is a medical photographer for St. Joseph's Hospital and the owner of Charles Ribbens Photography. Specializing in environmental, portrait, and corporate photography, Ribbens has exhibited his work at the William Scarbrough House in Savannah and the River Valley Playhouse and Art Center in Putney, Vermont.

KAREN ROEDER received a B.A. in art and a B.S. in biology from Armstrong State College in 1982. She has been a free-lance photographer and artist for 12 years, specializing in nature, documentary, scientific, and public relations photography. Her work has been featured in textbooks, journals, and various other educational publications.

JOSEPH SHIELDS is a free-lance photographer who specializes in landscape and location photography. He has received top awards in numerous regional, national, and international exhibitions and competitions. Shields' work has been published in *Coast, Savannah,* and *Savannah Scene* magazines, and will be included in *Best of Photography Annual: 1992.*

JOSEPH TROTZ is a *Savannah News-Press* photographer whose work has appeared in national and international publications, including *USA Today, Boston Globe, Vanity Fair,* and *The New York Times.* A graduate of Brandeis University in Waltham, Massachusetts, Trotz also has received several Associated Press and Georgia Press Association awards.

GREGORY WILLIAMS is a photographer for a local manufacturing company in Savannah. He produces work for advertising campaigns, instruction manuals, and promotional brochures. Williams also enjoys nature, abstract, and architectural photography. His work was included in an exhibition entitled, "Special Places in a Land Nearby," hosted by the Marine Extension Service of the University of Georgia.

An employee seems small in comparison with a reel of liner-board—which averages 60 to 70 tons—produced by Union Camp's newest paper machine, dubbed No. 8. The linerboard is cut to customer specifications before being transported.

JOSEPH BYRD

Index of Patrons

The Waving Girl Park on River Street honors Florence Martus, who was born on Cockspur Island in 1868 and moved to Elba Island in 1887. For the 44 years she lived on Elba Island with her brother, George, who was keeper of the lights of the Savannah River, she waved a white cloth by day and a lantern by night to ships passing by on the river. The Waving Girl received thousands of letters from lonely sailors, and, with her simple act of greeting, became the city's most enduring symbol of hospitality.